Anti-Catholicism in the Media

An examination of whether elite news organizations are biased against the Church

Edited by
Patrick Riley and Russell Shaw

Our Sunday Visitor Publishing Division
Our Sunday Visitor, Inc.
Huntington, Indiana 46750

Contents

II. The Conference

III. Historical Background

IV. Editors

Introduction

Patrick Riley and Russell Shaw

THIS BOOK PRESENTS to the American public a scientific study of the treatment given to the Catholic Church, to things Catholic, and to Catholics themselves by four titans of the American media: *The New York Times*, *The Washington Post*, *Time* magazine, and CBS News.

The sponsoring organizations, the Knights of Columbus and the Catholic League for Religious and Civil Rights, sought a study that would be as scientifically-based and objective as possible. That the Center for Media and Public Affairs has achieved this aim seems clear enough from the comments of a group of persons who met on September 17, 1991, at the National Press Club in Washington, D.C., to discuss the study, *Media Coverage of the Catholic Church*. Among them were two who hold highly responsible jobs in institutions scrutinized by the study: CBS News and *The Washington Post*.

The proceedings of the meeting are published here along with the text of *Media Coverage of the Catholic Church*.

Because an executive summary of *Media Coverage* is found at the beginning of that study, there is no need to summarize it here. What should be summarized are chief points and arguments that emerged in the discussion.

These professionals — journalists, media analysts,

organizational and "think tank" representatives, among others — understood perfectly well that the role of an analytical study such as *Media Coverage of the Catholic Church* is not to make judgments about the right way and wrong way to cover a religious institution such as the Catholic Church, but simply to isolate and analyze data that sketch the image of the Church as presented by the media. What emerged from the data and analysis was that the major media tend to present the Church as, for the most part, oppressive rather than liberating, irrelevant rather than relevant. The study itself was not called upon to pass judgment on the media. However, the principal author of the study, Dr. S. Robert Lichter, commented at the conference:

> If journalism in general has become negativistic and adversarial, does that justify or legitimize negative coverage of a religious institution? I think you have to make a decision about what appropriate coverage is, which transcends the scientific: that is, a value judgment about where the line of appropriate coverage lies.

That of course is what every reader of *Media Coverage of the Catholic Church* will do. It is certainly what most of the participants in the colloquy did. From the first speaker onward, the participants took sides without apology.

L. Brent Bozell III opened the conference by indicting the major media for shabby treatment of the Church, of Catholics, and of the things Catholics hold dear.

His respondent, Ambassador Frank Shakespeare, pointed to the openly Christian character of official discourse, both public and private, in earlier periods of our history. He provided vivid examples from Abraham Lincoln to Harry Truman. He contrasted the open piety of Presidents with the rigorous and indeed militant secularism of the present-day media, who denounced a

President for speaking in terms of the most basic moral concepts, namely good and evil.

As if to confirm Ambassador Shakespeare's point that recent civil discourse has been secularist, Richard Harwood of *The Washington Post* offered an historical explanation of the secularism of the press, as documented in *Media Coverage*. In the course of his explanation came a series of self-revelations rendered all the more striking by Mr. Harwood's reputation as the *Post*'s eminently fair ombudsman (at the time of this conference), and his claim to be no more than typical of journalists in the major media.

For example, Harwood called the age-old Catholic prohibition of contraception a "policy," as if it were a rule or regulation set by a legislature or administrative body, which could be adjusted or withdrawn at any time. The legalism underlying this also is reflected in the frequent use by the media of the term "ban" for the Church's condemnation of abortion.

It is little wonder that Mr. Harwood could speak of the "intrusion" of religion into secular affairs, or that he more than once used the term "secular" as if it meant secularist. Nor, in this perspective, is it surprising to find him claiming that journalists are free to write about the Church's teachings as if they had no more weight *within the Church* than political declarations have within the nation: ". . .as journalists we're under no obligation to give superior weight or credence to an institutional declaration the Pope declares, or the cardinals declare, or whatever."

The scene was set for a lively debate. It came quickly enough when Reed Irvine, chairman of Accuracy in Media, questioned Harwood on the *Post*'s tendency to seek comment from opponents of the Church's teachings. It is scarcely the business of the secular press to pass judgment on doctrinal matters, but, ideologically speaking, it may be the business of the *secularist* press. This distinction was for the most part ignored in the discussions, but it loomed large over them.

Another useful distinction can be drawn here. It lies between coverage by the media of the Church's inner activity, that is, the work of teaching and maintaining discipline, and coverage of the Church's activity in secular affairs.

Thomas F. Troy, president of the Washington Chapter of the Catholic League, complained that the Church is not admitted as an equal into civic discourse, but is treated by the media as an invader and potential usurper. He was replying not to Mr. Harwood, but to Professor Michael Robinson of Georgetown University, who criticized the statistical analysis presented in *Media Coverage of the Catholic Church* on grounds that it ignored what he deemed a favorable treatment of Catholicism in the entertainment media, and argued that both polls and election results proved that Catholics are highly regarded by the American people.

Professor Robinson received a formal point-by-point response from Kenneth Whitehead, former Assistant Secretary for Post-Secondary Education. He also got impromptu responses from Robert Royal, Vice President of the Ethics and Public Policy Center, and Michael McManus, a syndicated columnist specializing in religion.

McManus argued that the media pay much less attention to religion than is warranted by the interest that Americans have in it. Mr. McManus and Mr. Harwood proposed that the elite media, such as the four organs scrutinized in *Media Coverage of the Catholic Church*, are not representative of media across the country. Out there in Middle America, the dailies and the local TV and radio stations are much friendlier to religion in general, and the

Catholic Church in particular, than certain newsrooms in Washington and New York.

Yet the situation varies greatly from place to place and from case to case. And the argument overlooks the unique role of elite news organizations such as the four studied by Dr. Lichter and his co-workers. This role is twofold. First, elite media have a disproportionate influence on persons and groups in our society who wield power and are themselves positioned to shape public attitudes — for example, writers, academics, political leaders. Second, elite media also have a disproportionate influence on other news organizations and journalists. They set standards for the rest of the media, virtually determining how events and issues will be covered. Not least important for the coverage of religion is the tendency, documented by the Lichter study, of the major media to treat religious issues "along the familiar lines of political reportage."

We arrive at a curious anomaly, which on examination seems inevitable, given the preconceptions of the media elites. The elite secular media have come to see the inner life of the Church in political terms: ecclesiastical parties, personal rivalries, patronage. Within this optic, both moral and dogmatic teachings become mere policy. Yet these same secular media — or more precisely these same *secularist* media — sound the alarm when Catholic doctrine impacts on civil society, and especially when those responsible for teaching Catholic doctrine speak clearly, forcefully, and prophetically. And they voice alarm not only when the Church speaks clearly, forcefully, and prophetically to the world, but when she speaks thus to Catholics.

Do the data and the personal impressions brought together in this volume show a persistent practice of anti-Catholicism on the part of major secular media in the United States? Readers will judge for themselves.

There is, however, ample evidence here that Catholic dissent received copious and respectful attention from these media over the last three decades, while the beliefs and values of Catholics loyal to the magisterium of their Church did not fare so well. In the editors' view, that points to at least one major conclusion: The mindset dominant today in elite American media — call it secularism, call it the liberal zeitgeist, call it postmodern deconstructionist individualism — has found a better way to undermine the Catholic Church than was ever dreamed of by the old, religiously-inspired anti-Catholicism. It has learned to be selective and to reward Catholic dissent.

Participants in the Conference

Carl Anderson, Knights of Columbus
Mrs. Mary Ellen Bork, author and lecturer
L. Brent Bozell III, Media Research Center
Rev. Owen F. Campion, *Our Sunday Visitor*
Rev. Kenneth Doyle, National Conference of Catholic Bishops
  and United States Catholic Conference
Greg Erlandson, *Our Sunday Visitor*
Richard Harwood, *The Washington Post*
Brian Healy, CBS News
Reed Irvine, Accuracy in Media
Dr. S. Robert Lichter, Center for Media and Public Affairs
Robert Lockwood, *Our Sunday Visitor*
Michael McManus, syndicated columnist
Richard McMunn, *Columbia* magazine
Dr. Patrick Riley, Catholic League for Religious and Civil Rights
Dr. Michael J. Robinson, Georgetown University
Robert Royal, Ethics and Public Policy Center
Michael Schwartz, The Free Congress Foundation
Hon. Frank Shakespeare
Russell Shaw, Knights of Columbus
Thomas Troy, Catholic League for Religious and Civil Rights
David Wagner, Family Research Council
Hon. Kenneth D. Whitehead
Larry Witham, *The Washington Times*

I. The Study ✎

Media Coverage of the Catholic Church

The following text, pp. 12-137, was published by the Knights of Columbus and The Catholic League, © 1991, and was used as the basis for a symposium held in Washington, D.C. to discuss how major U.S. secular media cover the Catholic Church.

S. Robert Lichter, Daniel Amundson, and Linda S. Lichter

Executive Summary

THE PUBLIC IMAGE of social groups and institutions depends heavily on their portrayal in the news media. Given the long history of anti-Catholic prejudice in American society, it is especially important that the media present a fair and balanced portrayal of the Catholic Church. Most journalists approach the Church from an outsiders' perspective. A survey of national media outlets indicates that only one to two percent were practicing Catholics. But this need not prevent them from providing fair and balanced coverage of the Church. To address this issue, it is necessary to analyze the style and substance of actual news stories.

To provide an independent assessment of the media's performance, the Knights of Columbus and the Catholic League for Religious and Civil Rights commissioned a scientific study of news coverage by the Center for Media and Public Affairs. The study examined a sample of nationally influential media outlets (*The New York Times*, *The Washington Post*, *Time* magazine, and the CBS Evening News), during three 5-year time blocs: 1964-68, 1974-78, and 1984-88. The study focused on both news and editorial material that dealt with Catholic matters, primarily in the United States.

The analysis relied on the social-science method of content analysis. This technique allows researchers to classify the news objectively and systematically, and to produce valid measures of news content. The difference between content analysis and casual monitoring is akin to the difference between scientific polling and man-on-the-street interviews.

Trends in Coverage

On most controversies involving Catholic teachings, the Church came out on the losing side of the issue debate reported in the media. Although the opinion breakdown varied from one issue to another, sources supporting the Church were in the minority on the broad range of debates involving sexual morality and Church authority that dominated the coverage. These included heated controversies over birth control, clerical celibacy, the role of women and minorities in the Church, and its response to internal dissent and issues involving freedom of expression.

The major exception to this pattern involved ecumenical efforts, which the media treated as a kind of "motherhood and apple pie" issue, supported by all people of good will. Even on this dimension, however, opinion was split over whether the Church was helping or hindering efforts to promote interreligious unity. Similarly, opinion was about evenly divided on the Church's involvement in political affairs. But most of the praise was for Church pronouncements condemning war. On domestic disputes over church-state relations, most sources opposed the Church's positions or activities.

Controversial issues were frequently presented as conflicts between the Church hierarchy, on one side, and lower-level clergy, lay Catholics, and non-Catholics on the other. Journalists frequently approached this subject matter from a secular perspective, structuring their coverage of theological issues along the familiar lines of political reportage.

The result was a long-running media drama that pitted a hidebound institutional hierarchy against reformers from within and without. This portrayal was reinforced by the language used to describe the Church in media accounts. The descriptive terms most frequently applied to the Church emphasized its conservative theology, authoritarian forms of control, and anachronistic approach to contemporary society.

Moreover, long-term trends in the coverage have been unfavorable to the Church. Over time, official Church teachings were reported less frequently and were challenged more often when they did appear.

Among the four media outlets in the study, CBS focused most heavily on the papacy and least heavily on social conflicts involving the Church. By contrast, *Time* magazine paid the most attention to dissidents and focused most heavily on conflict, used judgmental language most frequently, and printed more opinions opposed to the Church than favorable on every issue except ecumenism.

Sexual Morality

The Church's teachings on sexual behavior were the leading topic of controversy in every time period and in three of the four outlets in the study. At *The Washington Post*, debate over sexual morals took second place to discussions of power relations within the Church.

Among all statements that clearly expressed their agreement or disagreement with Church teachings on these issues, about four out of seven disagreed with the Church. Church teachings on sexual morality were endorsed almost exclusively by members of the hierarchy; members of the laity and non-Catholics were overwhelmingly opposed. The overall effect was to present the debate over sexual morality as a split between the Church hierarchy and everyone else.

When discussing Catholic teaching on birth control, 53 percent of sources disagreed with the Church's stand against artificial contraception. As more and more polls indicated that American Catholics were not following the teaching, the subject was relegated to debate within the Church and news stories rarely quoted opinions from secular sources.

Priestly celibacy was one of the few areas of contention on which opinions did not change much over time, possibly because it was presented entirely as an internal debate among priests and their superiors.

Over time, positions on the Church's opposition to abortion shifted. During the 1970s most published statements supported the Church. This was due to the reiteration of the Catholic teaching by members of the hierarchy in response to the *Roe v. Wade* decision. By the 1980s, dissent had nearly doubled; the balance of opinion stood slightly against the Church. This can largely be attributed to secular groups stepping up their campaign for abortion rights and to a group of dissenting nuns and priests who made headlines with a *New York Times* ad requesting a change in Church policy. This prompted the Church to reassert its traditional teaching more frequently.

Church Authority and Dissent

The media gave heavy coverage to issues of power and authority within the Church. Opinions in news stories consistently favored decentralizing power. Support for change was almost twice as frequent as defense of the status quo. Defenders of the status quo were concentrated among the hierarchy. Once again the laity and clergy below the level of bishop lined up on the other side. Among non-Catholics opposition was almost unanimous, at 91 percent.

The Church's traditions came under attack with regard to both its treatment of constituent groups and its handling of dissent. Two out of three sources condemned its handling of dissenters in its ranks, and three out of four criticized its response to issues involving freedom of expression (such as academic freedom at Catholic universities). The only recurrent voices cited in defense of the status quo were again those of the Church hierarchy.

The 1970s saw a dramatic change in this arena of debate. Women's rights and status became the major point of contention. As racism and sexism loomed larger in debate, the Church was often attacked by secular sources.

The most dramatic rise in discussion during the 1980s came in the area of free expression. This was largely due to discussions of academic freedom and dissent connected to such high-profile figures as Father Charles Curran and Archbishop Raymond Hunthausen, along with Cardinal Joseph Ratzinger's push for greater theological orthodoxy. In this area Church decisions were rejected or criticized in 63 percent of all opinions.

Ecumenism and Church-State Relations

Overall, seven out of ten sources supported Church efforts to build unity and improve relations with other world religions. Even so, when debate arose over the Church's position on this widely approved goal, half the sources criticized the Church as an obstacle to greater unity.

Discussions of the Catholic Church's relations with various levels of government in the United States received the least coverage of any dimension in this study. Opinion was about evenly split, with 51 percent supporting the Church in its relations with government and 49 percent expressing some criticism. Over the course of time, however, opinion clearly turned against the Church. By the 1980s, those who supported the Church had dropped to a minority of only 40 percent.

Support for the Church's relations with the political world was bolstered by the Church's anti-war stance. On domestic concerns, by contrast — concerns such as public funding for private schools, the politics of abortion legislation, and perceived threats to the separation of church and state — few sources supported Church involvement in political affairs.

Church involvement in politics was always seen as an inappropriate threat to the separation of church and state. The margin of criticism increased in recent years. In the 1970s critics outnumbered supporters by a two-to-one margin, and in the 1980s the margin widened to three-to-one.

Descriptive Language

The media's depiction of the Church includes not only its presentation of policy issues, but also the tone of news accounts, which is strongly influenced by the use of descriptive language. A majority of stories employing descriptive language stressed the Church's conservatism, in all outlets and time periods studied. The tendency to emphasize the Church's conservatism increased during the

1970s. In addition, the Church was overwhelmingly portrayed as an oppressive or authoritarian institution. Over the course of time the Church was increasingly portrayed in this light. An institution that was usually described as conservative and oppressive was also presented more often than not as irrelevant. The Church's lack of relevance was emphasized more heavily in recent years. In sum, the linguistic tone of news coverage has been generally (and increasingly) unfavorable to the Church. At every outlet, and during every time period, it was usually portrayed as an oppressive or authoritarian institution with little relevance for the contemporary world.

Ultimately, journalists are less fact-collectors than story-tellers. And the stories they tell about the Catholic Church rely on politics as much as religion for their dramatic appeal. Increasingly, the story line revolves around a beleaguered authority struggling to enforce its traditions and decrees on a reluctant constituency.

Introduction

ANTI-CATHOLICISM HAS DEEP roots in American life. It arrived with the English settlers of the New World, who brought with them a deep suspicion of "Romanism" that became part of our Anglo-American heritage. During the nineteenth century the nativist movement added ethnic prejudice to religious conviction. In our own century, the political force of anti-Catholic feeling that helped defeat Al Smith in 1928 was still strong enough in 1960 to force John Kennedy to declare his political independence of Rome in an extraordinary speech to a gathering of Protestant clergymen.

In many respects, the problem of anti-Catholicism parallels that of anti-Semitism in America. In both cases, the suspicion of an alien religious tradition was allied to ethnic prejudice directed against successive waves of European immigrants whose native faith seemed to intensify their foreignness. Adherents of both religions have even had to face similar canards of dual loyalty — the one to Rome, the other to Tel Aviv. Ultimately, though, popular stereotypes of Jews are linked to their shared ethnicity. By contrast, Catholics of all ethnic and national backgrounds are defined by their adherence to a shared faith. This faith is embodied in a Church whose ritual, hierarchical structure, and claim to spiritual authority produce an unavoidable dissonance with the democratic and individualist tendencies of the American political culture, as well as our increasingly secularized public discourse.

In recent decades the more overt and virulent forms of anti-Catholicism have retreated from polite society and the public square, along with other forms of once fashionable religious and ethnic bigotry. In theory, the Catholic Church is now more able than ever before to compete for the hearts and minds of Americans within an atmosphere of religious tolerance. Yet Catholic anti-defamation organizations complain of a continuing bias that is all the more corrosive for its apparent lack of self-consciousness. As Michael Schwartz writes in *The Persistent Prejudice*, "Hostility to the Catholic Church functions as the unspoken premise for a great deal of what passes for the intellectual and cultural life of contemporary America."[1] Citing numerous examples of popular entertainment portrayals of Catholic clergy and doctrine, Schwartz concludes: "Catholicism is represented alternatively as ridiculous or cruel and oppressive. . . . The mass media image of Catholics is only slightly better than that of Nazis."[2]

Whatever the excesses of Hollywood, the Church's

relationship to the news media has proven even more problematic for both institutions. Both the news media and the Church are in the business of information gathering and dissemination. The Church provides information melded to interpretations based on doctrines it holds to be true and proper. The news media provide factual information and interpretation of its context and meaning without recourse to transcendent truths. For the journalist, balancing opinions on an issue, the credibility of sources, and concerns over legal formulas of fairness shape the presentation and analysis of information. These differing approaches inevitably lead to conflict between the two institutions. In assembling the news, the truth of Catholic teachings is opened to debate, just as the truths in a political speech are open to question.

Nonetheless, mainstream American journalists recognize an obligation to their own profession's canons of fairness and balance in reporting on the policies and activities of the Church, just as any other social institution. Few would dispute that most journalists approach the Church from an outsider's vantage point. My own 1980 survey of national media journalists at the television networks and the prestige press found that only 12 percent were Catholic, and 86 percent said they seldom or never attended religious services.[3] Interpolation from these two figures suggests that only one or two percent of major media journalists are practicing Catholics. Yet this does not necessarily imply a bias against the Church. Journalists are trained to cover individuals, issues, and institutions in a fair and impartial manner, regardless of their own relationship to the object of their coverage. The question is whether they succeed in doing so. And the answer must ultimately be found in an examination of their coverage rather than their personal backgrounds or beliefs.

Media Coverage of the Catholic Church

To analyze media coverage of the Catholic Church is a daunting task, owing to the sheer magnitude and diversity of the material under consideration. A comprehensive and systematic examination requires analysis of such issues as the prominence of the Church in news stories, the topics and sources involved in the coverage, characterizations of the behavior and policies of the Church, and opinions about Church teachings. Moreover, we wished to examine any changes that had occurred in the coverage over time. Therefore, our chosen study period extended back over a quarter century to 1964, encompassing coverage of the Church during the entire post-Vatican II era.

To reduce this task to manageable proportions, we concentrated on a sample of nationally influential media outlets which, previous research has shown, serve as opinion leaders for the journalistic profession in America. This sample included *The New York Times* and *The Washington Post*, which are the nation's most influential general-interest daily newspapers; *Time* magazine, the most venerable and widely read of the major newsweeklies; and the CBS Evening News, the flagship broadcast of what was for many years the nation's most prestigious and widely viewed broadcast news operation. In order to reduce further the number of stories to be considered, while permitting comparisons of coverage over time, we restricted the analysis to three five-year time blocs: 1964 through 1968, 1974 through 1978, and 1984 through 1988. This permits comparison of coverage through three different decades.

The study focused on news items that dealt with the Catholic Church in the United States. This included news about policy statements by the Vatican that would affect American Catholics, but not news that focused primarily on the Church's role in other countries. We defined news items to include both news and editorial material. The study included unsigned editorials and signed columns and op-ed pieces, but not letters to the editor (since these were produced by readers rather than journalists) or editorial cartoons (a different genre of expression).

During the fifteen years included in this sample frame, the four outlets studied ran over 10,000 news items about the Catholic Church in America (see table 1, p. 121). To obtain a representative example of this coverage, we examined: (1) all articles that appeared in *Time* magazine; (2) all stories that aired on the CBS Evening News beginning in 1974 (network news broadcasts were not collected in any publicly available archive until the late 1960s); (3) random samples of *The New York Times* and *The Washington Post*, necessitated by the much larger number of news items that appeared in these daily newspapers. We sampled ten percent of relevant articles at the *Times* and 20 percent at the *Post*. The difference reflected heavier news coverage of the Church in the *Times*.[4]

The final sample analyzed in the study numbered 1,876 news items. CBS aired 231 reports with a total airtime of five hours 54 min. (Again, this represents only the last two time blocs, for which broadcasts are publicly available for analysis.) *Time* magazine ran 260 stories totalling 4,274 column inches of text. Based on the random samples described above, 835 *The Washington Post* stories were included, which occupied 11,278 column inches of coverage. *The New York Times* sample totalled 550 articles with an accumulated total of 7,622 column inches.

Over the three time periods in our analysis, the number of stories and amount of space devoted to Catholicism dropped steadily. In the 1960s, when coverage was at its peak, the three print outlets contributed 771 stories to the sample, totalling 9,153 column inches of text. By the 1970s,

Media Coverage of the Catholic Church

the number of stories had dropped to 454, and total space declined to 7,229 column inches. The 1980s saw the coverage diminish further, to 420 articles totalling 6,792 column inches. CBS followed a similar trend, with coverage falling from 126 stories totalling 190 minutes of airtime during the 1970s to 105 stories totalling 164 minutes during the 1980s. Despite this downward trend, the average length of a story in all print outlets increased over time by more than 25 percent, climbing from under 12 column inches during the 1960s to over 16 inches in the 1980s. As a result, the later stories contributed proportionately more material to the study.

This sample contained only 64 signed or unsigned opinion articles, representing three percent of all news items. Moreover, the editorial material did not differ significantly or systematically from the much larger pool of news reports in its topical focus or distribution of opinion. The few exceptions to this pattern are noted in the text.

Research Method

OUR ANALYSIS OF news about the Catholic Church relied on the social science method of content analysis. This technique allows researchers to classify the news objectively and systematically according to explicit rules and clear criteria. The goal is to produce valid measures of news content, and the hallmark of success lies in reliability. Other investigators who apply similar procedures to the same material should obtain similar results, although their interpretations of those results may differ. Clear rules and standards have to be set for identifying, measuring, and classifying each story. In making each decision, coders must be applying rules, not expressing their own opinions. If the rules are sufficiently clear, two coders working independently will come to the same conclusions, regardless of their own opinions about the subject matter.

Content analysis is not a panacea. The quality of a study depends on the way the coding categories are constructed, the clarity and appropriateness of the rules that guide coders in applying them, and the skill of the coders in doing so. Nonetheless, the difference between content analysis and casual monitoring is akin to the difference between scientific polling and man-on-the-street interviews.

There are two basic forms of content analysis. Quantitative analysis measures specified messages in numerical terms. It presupposes the existence of well defined, mutually exclusive categories, which are used to examine the data. Qualitative analysis, sometimes referred to as thematic or emergent analysis, involves non-numerical procedures. It usually lacks the specified and defined categories of quantitative analysis. These two forms of research complement and supplement each other.

When exploring new territory where existing coding categories may not apply, researchers first employ qualitative techniques. This involves canvassing the universe of content to be examined. Extensive notes are taken on each item dealing with substance, style, and format. After this is completed, the notes are compared to see what common themes, symbols, and attributes emerge. From this information, the researchers develop the categories that are eventually employed in the quantitative analysis. These qualitative techniques help research to become "data sensitive" by developing categories that specifically accommodate the research material. Emergent analysis also allows researchers to record qualitative examples that can be used later to illustrate the quantitative categories.

Our research strategy combined these two approaches.

The first phase employed a qualitative emergent analysis to conceptualize and operationalize the system, based on prior examination of a wide range of news stories. Rather than imposing preordained categories on the material, they emerged from an extensive pilot study of a diverse set of media outlets. Once the analytic categories were developed and pre-tested, they became the basis of the second research phase, the quantitative analysis presented in this report. This involved the systematic coding of the story content into discrete categories that are subject to numerical representation and, hence, quantitative data manipulation.

For this project, two coders spent four months in training to learn all of the categories and arrive at reliable decisions. A minimum reliability level of 80 percent was achieved for all variables retained in the final analysis. Agreement on most variables was considerably higher. Throughout the coding process, coders were randomly assigned stories to reduce systematic error further. The results of this analysis provide the basis for the report that follows.

In order to make the process of content analysis easier to understand, consider the following *New York Times* story, which appeared in the sample. This story was not chosen because it was typical of all *New York Times* stories, but rather because it illustrates how our analysis works in breaking down the news into measurable components.

... For a 'New Age' Priest

By Jane Gross

Special to the New York Times

1 San Francisco, Oct. 20 — An obscure Roman Catholic priest, popular on the New Age lecture circuit, but about to be silenced by the Vatican, today cast himself in the mold of Galileo, St. Thomas Aquinas and other Catholics who have been disciplined over the centuries by the Church hierarchy.

2 The Rev. Matthew Fox offered an impassioned defense of his attitudes and actions at a news conference. **He confirmed recent press reports** that he had been investigated by the Vatican's Congregation for the Doctrine of the Faith, which, under the leadership of Joseph Cardinal Ratzinger, has been increasingly vigilant about doctrinal diversity.

3 "There is an honor attached to being silenced by the present regime in the Vatican," said Father Fox, the 47-year-old founder of the institute in Culture and Creation Spirituality, an avant garde master's degree program at Holy Names College in Oakland. Reciting the names of other Catholics who have been disciplined, he added, "One might even get the impression from a litany such as this that the Roman Catholic Church's track record on just who to silence among its most prophetic voices is not overwhelmingly impressive."

'A Period of Reflection'

4 Father Fox, a Dominican, said that his order, supportive throughout a four-and-a-half year investigation, has asked him to cease preaching, lecturing and teaching for a year at the insistence of the Vatican. In Rome, the procurator general of the Dominican order, the Rev. Rafael Moya, confirmed that Father Fox had been asked, "in accord with the Vatican", to "observe a period of reflection.". . .

5 Father Fox's institute, which enrolls about 100 students each year at a tuition of $7,500, seems like an unlikely tenant at Holy Names College, a 120-year-old liberal arts school in the wooded hills overlooking Oakland and the San Francisco Bay. . . .

6 Today the college president, Sister Lois MacGillivray, said that Father Fox had requested and been granted a one semester sabbatical, effective December 15. The institute will continue to operate in his absence, she said, and the college will consider extending the sabbatical if Father Fox requests it. . . .

Criticized by Conservatives

7 The institute has long been the object of criticism by conservative Catholics for its unusual curriculum and faculty, which includes a masseuse, a yoga instructor, an Episcopal vicar turned Zen Buddhist and a self described witch, Starhawk. . . .

8 The letter from Cardinal Ratzinger also instructs that Father Fox "cease from further dissemination of the central thesis" of the most popular of his 12 books, "Original Blessing." The book quarrels with the "over-emphasis" on original sin in Catholic theology at the expense of a more positive focus. *Father Fox said he had also been criticized for espousing the ordination of women and for speaking to gay audiences.*

9 At his news conference today, Father Fox predicted that the Vatican's disciplinary action would stimulate interest in the philosophy of his institute. "Perhaps things like this are providential," he said. "If you look at the history of the Church, overreaction to new movements has been like pouring gasoline on a fire."

10 *At the same time, however, he lashed out at the Church which he described as a dying patriarchy that commits acts of "institutional violence" every time it "silences theologians rather than engaging them in dialogue."*

11 "The Vatican keeps telling us that the Church is not a democracy," Father Fox said. "I know of no one who would argue that point. But maybe the church ought to be. Did Jesus intend a monarchy? Did Jesus intend a fascist state?" (10/21/88)

What information does this story convey about Catholicism, and how can it be categorized? The most obvious characteristics of this report concern its topic, sources, presentation of opinions, and use of emotive language. Beginning in paragraphs 1 and 2, it is clear that the topic of the story is dissent within the Church. Paragraphs 3 and 8 add evidence that this is dissent from a liberal direction. Thus its topical focus would be coded as liberal dissent. When we examine the remainder of the story, there are no other topics discussed in sufficient depth to be coded.

Paragraph 2 also provides the first source citation in the story (indicated in bold). All other sources in this excerpt are highlighted to make them easier to identify. Father Fox was coded as a Dominican, as was Father Moya. Sister MacGillivray was identified as a member of a religious order for women. Cardinal Ratzinger, a frequent news source, was assigned his own individual coding number. This makes it possible to classify all of his quotations along the dimensions identified by our coding system. Notice that some sources are quoted verbatim while others are paraphrased by the reporter. Regardless of the convention employed, however, all of these statements are directly attributed to a particular source.

In order to determine how the story presents Church teachings, we must examine the entire article. From paragraph 2 we know that a member of the Church hierarchy expresses his views. Reading down to paragraph 8, we find ideas identified as the view of the Church on Father Fox's teachings. Because of the content of paragraphs 2, 8, and 10, we would identify this story as one containing an official Church doctrine. Since it is also clear that Father Fox disagrees with the Church, we would code this as a story that debates Church teachings.

Father Fox's quote at the end of paragraph 8 (see italics) presents his support for the ordination of women but does not hold any explicit opinion on his views toward homosexuality. The article merely mentions that he has addressed gay groups, not that he supports their cause. For our coding system, it was essential that an opinion be clearly stated and not inferred from context or the official position of the speaker.

In paragraph 10 (see italics) Father Fox's reaction to Vatican disciplinary moves yields another viewpoint. Here he clearly criticizes the Church for cracking down on doctrinal diversity, terming it "institutional violence." He would be coded as critical of the Church's handling of dissent.

To determine how language is used to characterize the Church, we must search for the use of particular terms. The reference to "conservative Catholics" in paragraph 7 yields the first example of how descriptive terms were used in news stories. Other more emotive or judgmental terms characterizing the Church can be found in paragraphs 10 and 11, with the terms "patriarchy," "monarchy," and "fascist state." The term "conservative" causes the story to be coded as presenting a description of political ideology. The terms "patriarchy," "monarchy," and "fascist state" lead the story to be coded for the use of language characterizing the Church's exercise of authority as authoritarian or oppressive.

To dissect this story in such great detail may seem to labor the obvious. But it is necessary to illustrate how a news item can be broken into its constituent elements in a systematic and reliable fashion. In this case, a casual reader of the article would likely (but not necessarily) come away with an unfavorable overall impression of the Church, based on the article's attention to the charges of a dissident priest. Our analysis replaces such holistic impressions with more precise measurements of the article's topics, sources, structure, language, and opinions presented. The data we collect on this story would show that it presents a debate over Church policies on internal dissent, that the Church's policies are criticized, and that the Church is characterized as oppressive.

Moreover, these data can be combined with comparable data from the other 1,875 stories in the sample to provide an overall portrait of how the Church is presented along each dimension. These findings can then be desegregated to determine differences over time, among different media outlets, etc. In this way, the structure, tone, and balance of the coverage can be systematically assessed, rather than inferred from casual impressions based on subjective responses to an unrepresentative sample of news items.

Topics

WE BEGIN THIS discussion with an outline of the major topics of discussion in stories about the Catholic Church. Much of the news about any institution will be uncontroversial, and the Church is no exception. The factual, straightforward, and nonpartisan recounting of daily events provides the backdrop for the more interpretive or "politicized" accounts that draw charges of biased or unfair reporting. Readers tend to take the former for granted, while the latter stand out in sharp relief. Thus, the largest number of news stories over the years have concerned themselves with announcements of parish events, promotions of clergy and the accomplishments of outstanding Catholics (see table 2, p. 121). In our sample a total of 550 stories were related to these routine matters of Church business. That means nearly three out of every ten stories (29 percent) dealt with intrinsically non-controversial topics.

The following excerpt from a *New York Times* article is typical of these routine announcements and illustrates just how matter-of-fact they can be:

New Chief of Schools Selected for Archdiocese
Connors to Succeed Rigney in Superintendent's Post
By Gene Currivan

Msgr. Edward M. Connors, who has been associate superintendent of schools for the Roman Catholic Archdiocese of New York for the last nine years, has been named superintendent to succeed Msgr. Raymond P. Rigney.

The formal announcement of the change will be made today by Archbishop Terence J. Cooke.

Monsignor Rigney, who has been superintendent since 1964 and has been associated with the central office of education for 23 years, has been appointed pastor of the Church of St. Ann, 3511 Bainbridge Avenue, the Bronx.

As superintendent, Monsignor Connors will supervise the administration of 432 schools and 210,000 pupils in an area that covers Manhattan, the Bronx and Staten Island and seven upstate counties. The Brooklyn and Queens schools are administered by the diocese of Brooklyn.

The new head of the system, who grew up in the Bronx and is 47 years old, is the son of the late Edward Connors, who was chief of the New York City Fire Department until his death in 1959, the year that Monsignor Connors was named associate superintendent of schools.

He holds a Master of Arts degree and a doctorate from the Catholic University of America. His doctoral dissertation was entitled "Church-State Relations in Education in New York." (12/4/68)

The proportion of such routine announcements among church news remained stable over the years (see table 3, p. 122). In the 1960s, they represented 31 percent of all stories; during the 1970s 28 percent; and during the 1980s 29 percent. There was also little difference among outlets in this regard (see table 4, p. 123). In the pages of *Time*, *The Washington Post*, and *The New York Times*, about three out of ten stories covered routine events. On CBS the proportion was slightly lower (26 percent of all news).

News about the Pope finished a distant second, with 229 stories discussing the selection process or personal characteristics. Despite the fact that most major media journalists are not practicing Catholics, they can sometimes convey a positive image of the Church's spiritual leader. For example, a *Washington Post* column by Haynes Johnson was unusually effervescent in his admiration for the late John XXIII.

Faith

Only once in my lifetime has a Pope seemed anything other than impersonal. All other times he's been a character in some remote medieval pageant who makes an occasional brief appearance wrapped in splendor amid muted ceremony, and then quickly disappears from sight and mind.

I say that as a non-Catholic, but I suspect that many younger members of the faith feel the same way. Even in Rome, I know young Italians often are in the habit of referring to the pontiff as something of an irrelevance. "Papa," they remark: Papa will take care of this or that. They say it with an air of humorous affection mixed with a certain sardonic cynicism.

The exception was both notable and memorable. Not for 624 years had a pope had the name John, but when the portly figure of John XXIII entered the world stage in 1958 my perception of the papal office and the potentiality of its role changed.

Other popes of memory had even looked alike — austere, ascetic, unsmiling, pale, solemn and slim — men suited to the private chambers rather than the private corridors. John XXIII was of a different mold. With his jowls and prominent Roman nose and look of suppressed laughter about his eyes he exuded warmth and humanity. John was a good friar, jovial and affable, who cherished good living; he possessed the gifts of affection and compassion; he was open and accessible and conveyed a sense of welcome to all. . . . (8/9/78)

Of course, even such a positive portrayal illustrates the secular standpoint from which Johnson writes, as well as the tendency to base judgments on presumed personality characteristics. It is the stereotypical jovial "good friar" who overcomes the reporter's sense of emotional and spiritual distance from "a character in some remote medieval pageant."

Most stories discussing the Pope ran in the 1970s, a period that saw the selection of two popes. In the 1960s, far fewer stories discussed the Pope and his personal life, falling all the way to eighth among news topics. Much of the attention to the papacy during the 1960s occurred in retrospectives on the life of John XXIII and biographies of the recently elected Paul VI.

During the 1970s the number of stories about papal selection nearly doubled. Papal news in the 1970s was clustered in 1978 around the death of Pope Paul. The selection of John Paul I under new rules devised by Pope Paul added to interest in the process. The death of John

Paul I and the selection of a non-Italian to serve as John Paul II increased attention to happenings in the Vatican. In the 1980s, the attention given to the Pope dropped in absolute terms, while remaining the second most common news topic. Much of this attention was connected to John Paul's extensive travels and some residual concerns over the attempt made on his life in 1981.

CBS provided the heaviest coverage of the Pope in both absolute and proportional terms. The network aired 94 stories on the Pope, accounting for over 40 percent of all CBS stories. This undoubtedly reflects television's preference for spectacle, for choreographed events (such as papal visits), and for major newsmakers who are also institutional leaders. Thus, television's attention to the Pope is the functional equivalent of its attention to the President. *Time* magazine ran the fewest stories (32) but they represented one out of every eight Church-related stories in that weekly publication. The two newspapers gave the Pope proportionally even less coverage. At *The Washington Post* news about the Pope accounted for eight percent of Church-related stories. At *The New York Times* such articles represented only six percent of the news.

Catholic relations with other religions appears next on the list of most discussed topics. Over the entire sample period 176 stories addressed concerns over ecumenism or other aspects of relations between the Roman Catholic Church and some other religion. Ecumenism was largely a subject of discussion in the 1960s, with the reforms and attitudes of the Second Vatican Council leading the way. Eleven percent of stories in the 1960s dealt with inter-religious relations. These accounted for almost half (47 percent) of all discussions of ecumenism found in the study.

Catholic-Jewish relations received a boost in the 1960s with the Council's decision to exonerate modern day Jews of charges of deicide previously levelled against them. An often heated debate between Jewish and Catholic leaders over alleged sins of omission by the Church during the Holocaust, however, cast a cloud over this spirit of ecumenism. Pope Paul was more successful in mending fences with the Patriarchs of the Eastern Orthodox Church, culminating in a joint meeting on the Mount of Olives at Easter 1964 and their mutual retraction of excommunication orders. Catholic-Protestant relations improved greatly with efforts on a joint Bible and other theological discussions yielding greater understanding and cooperation.

The 1970s held less discussion of ecumenism. The debate over alleged Catholic complicity in the Holocaust continued, although general Catholic-Jewish relations were stable. Rapprochement with the Eastern Orthodox Church did not last, and increasing tensions threatened to chill the relationship. The Church also slowed those ecumenical efforts with Protestant churches, which it felt reduced or denigrated the uniqueness of the Catholic Church. This restriction took away much of the exuberance for ecumenism found in the 1960s.

In the 1980s, much of the news about inter-church relations marked new or continuing tensions in relations between faiths. New disputes over the Holocaust, a convent at Auschwitz and the visit of Kurt Waldheim to the Vatican troubled Catholic-Jewish relations. In 1989, *The New York Times* published an op-ed piece that confronted this downturn from a Jewish perspective:

Cardinal Ratzinger Cured Jews of an Illusion
By Arthur Hertzberg

Several weeks ago, yet another crisis broke out in the stormy recent history of Roman Catholic-Jewish relations. Joseph Cardinal Ratzinger, the chief theologian of the Vatican, asserted in an interview that a Jew encounters the full faith of his Judaism only by becoming a Catholic.

The Jewish partners in the formal dialogue between the two communities that began in 1971 immediately cancelled the next regularly scheduled meeting. Several Jewish representatives pronounced the dialogue to be impossible on Cardinal Ratzinger's terms.

But is it? I think not. Indeed, these are the only terms on which the church and the synagogue can really talk to each other. Cardinal Ratzinger has cured us of an illusion — that the church and the synagogue can negotiate a new, liberal theology on which both can agree. The fact is each has a different theological perspective and in theory the chasm is unbridgeable.

Cardinal Ratzinger's most recent statements are but another indication that the church of John Paul II is unhappy with much of the legacy of John XXIII. That revolutionary Pope had gone a long way toward dealing with other faiths, and especially Judaism, as precious and equal truths. The Vatican for which Cardinal Ratzinger speaks is insisting on asserting its religious primacy in the world. . . . (12/22/87)

Interreligious relations received the most attention at *The Washington Post* and *The New York Times*, representing about 11 percent of their total coverage, compared to eight percent at *Time* and only three percent at CBS.

Dissent in the Church was another major source of news across all three decades, accounting for seven percent of all topics discussed. Dissent from a liberal or radical direction attracted over five times as much coverage as conservative or reactionary dissent (138 vs. 26 stories).

Time magazine and *The Washington Post* provided the heaviest coverage of dissent. The following excerpt from a *Time* article typifies the coverage of liberal dissent:

Rome Sends a Strong Message
Chastised for dissent, a U.S. theologian loses his teaching license

Pope John Paul II began his reign eight years ago, at a time when theologians and laity alike were openly questioning some traditional teachings of the church. Since then the Vatican has attempted to restore a sense of doctrinal discipline; it removed renegade Swiss Theologian

Hans Küng from his teaching post at the University of Tubingen in West Germany and silenced for a year Brazilian Franciscan Leonardo Boff, an advocate of Marxist-tinged liberation theology. Last week Rome moved against an American priest who has openly questioned the church's stance on sexual morality. Joseph Cardinal Ratzinger, head of the Vatican's Congregation for the Doctrine of the Faith, revoked the license of the Reverend Charles Curran to teach theology at the Catholic University of America because of the priest's "repeated refusal to accept what the church teaches." The Vatican's long expected crackdown on Curran made it clear that the Pope will not tolerate open dissent on the part of those who claim to be the church's teachers. But some Roman Catholics were alarmed by what they called "creeping infallibilism" in Ratzinger's letter to Curran — that is, an attempt by Rome to place more and more of its official teachings beyond dispute.

At a Washington press conference last week, Curran insisted that the church, not he, "ultimately should change its teachings" and vowed to fight to retain his position at the university. Archbishop James Hickey of Washington, the chancellor of the university, has set a Sept. 1 deadline for Curran to decide whether to appeal through the school's own grievance procedures. . . . (9/1/86)

Most reports on dissension within the Church appeared in the 1960s, when 70 stories covered liberal critiques and 11 addressed conservative arguments. This is the period when critics like Hans Küng and Charles Curran rose to prominence through their attacks against Church teachings on birth control, abortion, the ordination of women and other issues. Other radical priests criticized the Church for its stands on the war in Vietnam, its reaction to poverty and economic injustice, and its record on civil rights. News accounts in the 1960s also followed conservative dissent, such as Father DePauw's Catholic Traditionalist Movement, which rejected changes in the liturgy and other reforms of Vatican II.

In the 1970s, dissent fell from fifth to tenth place on the news agenda. News about dissent dropped to less than three percent of all topics. Many of the old points of dissension, such as birth control, celibacy, and changes in the liturgy, were fading as topics. Thus, dissenters in these areas received less attention. Their place in the news agenda was taken over by new arguments about Church stands on abortion, which were often presented by critics from outside the Church.

News coverage of dissent made a comeback in the 1980s, rising to third on the agenda, ahead of all topics except for papal news and church happenings. Critics on the left became even more prominent, generating eight times as much coverage as their counterparts on the right. In the 1980s Father Curran was once again at the center of controversy, as the Church took strong disciplinary action against his controversial views. Other liberal or progressive minded priests also found themselves facing disciplinary action, as Cardinal Ratzinger re-emphasized orthodoxy. There was also a resurgence of right wing dissent covered by the news media. This was largely connected to Archbishop Lefebvre in France, so only a few of these stories appeared in our sample.

The outlets in the study differed on the attention they gave to dissent in the Church. *Time* magazine provided the heaviest proportional focus on dissent, at ten percent of the newsweekly's topical discussions. Dissent in the Church represented seven percent of all topics discussed in the *The Washington Post* and six percent in *The New York Times*. CBS trailed well behind, with dissent appearing in only ten stories, which accounted for three percent of topical discussions. Thus, dissent occupied only about half as much coverage of the Church at CBS as at the nation's leading newspapers.

Education and the Catholic Church is a multifaceted topic. It includes such issues as the quality of Catholic schooling, its importance in the modern age, concerns over the financial health of schools, legal challenges to school policies, the tensions between public and private educational systems, and labor problems that disrupted education. A total of 150 stories in the sample discussed some aspect of Church-related educational issues.

The following excerpt from a *New York Times* story is typical of coverage of labor disputes that threatened to disrupt Catholic education.

St. John's Dispute Could Branch Out, Union Leader Says

The Rev. Peter O'Reilly, leader of the faculty group that has called a Jan. 3 strike against St. John's University, warned yesterday that the dispute could spread to other Roman Catholic colleges across the country.

Asked if the unrest at St. John's could be a catalytic agent, he said: "There's an explosion coming and nothing is going to stop it."

Father O'Reilly, chairman of the St. John's chapter of the United Federation of College Teachers, is one of 31 faculty members dismissed for "unprofessional conduct" in the dispute over tenure and academic freedom. . . . (12/27/65)

Education was frequently discussed in the 1960s, when debates over educational quality as well as labor disputes made news. From a high of 68 stories in the 1960s, coverage fell to 43 and then 39 stories over the next two decades. Over the course of time legal changes resolved some of the labor disputes and established procedures for the resolution of future disputes. Additionally, while schools continued to face financial challenges and many closed, this trend drew less media attention.

Because of the general downward bend in coverage of the Church, however, education held its place about midway in the top ten topics throughout the three decades studied. Owing to its distinctly local flavor, education received proportionally heavier coverage at the *Post* and

Times, where it accounted for nine percent of stories, compared to seven percent at *Time* and two percent at CBS.

Discussion of Church regulation, particularly changes to the basic operating rules of the Church, was the sixth most discussed topic in the study. This discussion was largely driven by decisions made at the Second Vatican Council. The changes enacted regarding the vernacular Mass and other aspects of the liturgy; the role of the laity in running their church and ministering to their fellow man; and the role of priests, bishops, and cardinals in the power structure of the Church were all frequently covered areas of discussion.

Time magazine discussed some of the changes that had been approved and many of the more far-ranging proposals in the following article from 1966:

Roman Catholics Reforming Canon Law

Pope Paul called the Second Vatican Council "the beginning not the end" of renewal in the Roman Catholic Church, but apart from the vernacular liturgy, change has come slowly. To get on with reform, a study group of the Canon Law Society of America — representing the U.S. experts who teach and explain the church's juridical code — met this month in Pittsburgh and put forth a series of recommendations for carrying out the spirit of Vatican II.

The proposals, which emphasize human rights rather than church discipline, deal not only with the canon law code but with basic constitutional problems of the church. . . . .

Other proposals:

Abolition of all prior censorship of books (by withholding the imprimatur), and all outmoded ecclesiastical penalties, such as automatic excommunication without prior hearing for violation of the seal of confession.

Public justice, whenever possible as compared with the present star-chamber proceedings.

"Full participation" of women in the life of the Church — which some canonists interpret as a veiled recommendation that women be ordained to the priesthood.

> More allowance for local variation in applying a legal code that now attempts to be universal in scope. As one canonist foresees it, church law in the U.S. might some day use some of the procedures of English common law rather than those of the more codified Roman Law that underlies the existing canons. . . .(10/28/66)

A total of 136 stories discussed these and other aspects of the Church's procedural rules. The coverage dropped sharply from its peak of 95 stories in the 1960s to 33 reports in the 1970s and finally only 8 articles in the 1980s. Even the discussion in the 1970s was frequently connected to Vatican II, as Church officials struggled to implement mandated changes. There were many questions left to be resolved about how the laity or bishops were to share in the power of the Church, and many newsworthy disputes resulted.

CBS showed the least interest in these debates, while *Time* gave them proportionally the greatest coverage. CBS aired only five stories on changes in Church regulations, or two percent of all the Catholic-related stories the network aired. *Time*, on the other hand, devoted 17 percent of its coverage to these changes in Church structure and ritual. The magazine printed 44 stories, only slightly behind the 49 stories appearing in *The Washington Post*. The *Post* may have printed more stories, but that total represents only six percent of its coverage. *The New York Times* printed 38 stories, which accounted for seven percent of the total sample of stories there.

Two very controversial issues appear next in the topical discussions: birth control and abortion. Birth control was number seven in the order of discussion and appeared in 132 stories. Abortion was not far behind, with 104 stories discussing the Church stand against abortion.

Birth control became a major issue for the media in the 1960s with the publication of *Humanae Vitae*. On July 30, 1968 *Humanae Vitae* made the front page of *The New York Times*. This article is unusual in that it presents the

Church announcement of the encyclical with only minimal dissent. In this case the dissenting voices had their own adjoining article in which to voice their disapproval.

Pope Bars Birth Control By Any Artificial Means; Takes Note of Opposition
Tone Forthright
Encyclical Binding on Catholics but Is not Immutable Dogma
by Robert C. Doty

Five years of uncertainty over how the Roman Catholic Church would view modern methods of birth control ended today with the official presentation of a papal encyclical letter that upheld the prohibition on all artificial means of contraception.

The 7,500 word declaration by Pope Paul VI, "Humanae Vitae" ("Of Human Life"), reaffirmed that Roman Catholics might limit the size of their families only by the rhythm method — confining sexual intercourse to a woman's infertile period — or by abstinence.

This, it was conceded by both the Pontiff and Msgr. Ferdinando Lambruschini, the Lateran University moral theologian who presented the text at a news conference, "will perhaps not be easily received by all."

'Great Act of Courage'

But, the monsignor said, "in its human aspect the pontifical decision, which concedes nothing to popularity, is a great act of courage and perfect serenity."

In the opinion of other Roman churchmen, the Pope's decision, overruling the recommendations for liberalization by a majority of his own study commission of clerics and laymen and running counter to widespread pressure for change inside and outside the church, may produce a serious crisis of authority. . . .

Eighty percent of the stories we examined on birth control (106 out of 132) appeared between 1964 and 1968. This topic appeared in one out of every seven stories on the Church in the 1960s sample. The very spirited debate within the Church over the encyclical was quickly joined by secular forces who were concerned over its effect on world food shortages. Attention to this topic dropped sharply to only 18 reports in the 1970s and eight articles in the 1980s. This drop in media coverage coincided with the release of several polls (also reported in the media) indicating that large majorities of American Catholics were ignoring Church teaching on birth control. As the controversy attained what many took to be a de facto resolution domestically, it ceased to be newsworthy.

The three print outlets were roughly equal in the proportion of coverage given to birth control. Nine percent of the stories in *Time* dealt with the Church prohibition on artificial birth control, as did eight percent at both *The Washington Post* and *The New York Times*. CBS fell far behind, with only one percent of its stories addressing birth control. The virtual absence of coverage on CBS is largely due to its inclusion in the study for only the last two time periods, when the birth control debate was on the wane.

Media discussion of abortion did not really begin until midway through the study period. Then the coverage jumped nearly tenfold, from six stories in the 1960s sample to 57 in the 1970s. Interest remained high throughout the 1980s, as the last period in our sample generated 41 more stories. This increase was fueled by the Supreme Court's *Roe v. Wade* decision legalizing abortion and the subsequent increase in anti-abortion activities by the Church. For example, one year after the 1973 *Roe* decision, *The Washington Post* ran an article detailing the delicate nexus between the Church, politicians and the public, while also detailing disagreement within the Church over how to deal with this divisive issue.

Abortion, Congress, Churches, Convictions
By Marjorie Hyer

Two days after Spiro T. Agnew resigned, Delaware Sen. Joseph Biden, Jr. received 35 telegrams from his constituents with proposals for Agnew's successor as Vice President. All but one expressed strong opposition to then New York Gov. Nelson Rockefeller.

Clues to the source of this remarkable disaffection in the grass roots of Delaware for the governor of New York lay in the signatures to two of the telegrams: a Roman Catholic convent of the Sisters of Charity and the Delaware Right to Life Committee.

Two years earlier, Rockefeller had vetoed a bill that anti-abortion forces, spearheaded by Catholics, had urged through the state legislature. The measure was designed to overturn a year-old law making New York the first state in which any woman who so desired could get a hospital supervised abortion.

Today marks the first anniversary of a Supreme Court decision that, in effect, lifted all legal restraints on abortion in the early months of pregnancy.

If the seven Justices who were part of the majority decision in that case had any idea that they were settling, once and for all, national policy on this highly emotional question, they were seriously in error.

If anything the Court's decision has stimulated more activity than ever on the issue. . . .

In March, St. Joseph's College, a small Catholic school in North Windham, Maine, cancelled the honorary degree it had planned to give syndicated columnist Ann Landers because she "supports abortion."

(A month later, widely respected priest-psychologist Eugene Kennedy, in protest, sent back the honorary degree St. Joseph's had awarded him earlier. Praising the columnist for her sensitivity to Catholic views in general, Father Kennedy said: "We've never insisted that everybody should agree with everything we say in a pluralistic society.") . . . (1/22/74)

CBS, which lagged behind in covering many other aspects of Church life, gave proportionally the most coverage to this highly political and conflictual story. Twenty-two broadcasts, or ten percent of all CBS stories on the Catholic Church, dealt with abortion. This relatively heavy coverage reflects television's attraction to the drama and visual interest of abortion-related rallies and marches. By comparison, only seven percent of *The New York Times* stories on Church-related matters discussed abortion, as did five percent of all *Time* articles and four percent of *The Washington Post* stories.

Ninth on the list of most frequently discussed topics were civil rights issues. A total of 86 stories discussed the Church's involvement in civil rights. Social changes drew the Church most heavily into civil rights issues in the 1960s, when the issue generated 53 stories. These included pieces discussing activities by Catholic clergy to increase integration and tolerance, complaints that some church or diocese was racist in excluding or downgrading the participation of blacks and Hispanics, and Church statements that it was opposed to racism in any form.

A *Washington Post* article from 1968 typifies the fairly common presentation of Church efforts to foster civil rights.

St. Patrick's Address
Cardinal Asks Racial Justice

Irish Americans must be prepared to grant the Negroes and Puerto Ricans the same privileges their ancestors sought in the days when "No Irish Need Apply" signs hung outside business firms, Patrick Cardinal O'Boyle said last night on St. Patrick's Eve.

He told the Society of the Friendly Sons of St. Patrick, celebrating its 40th anniversary in the Statler-Hilton Hotel, that, "if our zeal for justice for the Negro, the Puerto Rican and Mexican is not sincere, then we have no right to complain of the injustices that our own forebears suffered years ago.". . . (3/17/68)

Coverage dropped sharply to 15 stories in the 1970s and 18 articles ten years later. (The sample did not extend far enough into the late 1980s to cover the recent debate over the accusations and claims of Father George Stallings about racism in the Church.) Civil rights concerns received their heaviest coverage in the newspapers. The *Post* and the *Times* covered civil rights issues in six percent of their Church-related stories, while CBS and *Time* magazine both covered civil rights concerns much more rarely, in only two percent of their stories.

Rounding out the list of the top ten most discussed topics was the debate over the Church's involvement in secular politics. This topic was only addressed seven times in the 1960s and did not make the top ten list for that era. In the 1970s, as the Church discouraged the clergy from holding political office, and was increasingly embattled over abortion and public funding for private schools, the line between church and state was more frequently debated. Our sample contained 40 stories that followed these debates during the 1970s. The 1980s saw only a slight reduction in the level of coverage, to 36 stories.

These discussions were highlighted by two different battles: public policy on abortion and diplomatic recognition of the Holy See by the United States government. The abortion coverage centered on statements by Cardinal O'Connor and other Catholic leaders that Catholic politicians were bound by the moral teachings of their church to outlaw abortion. Many of the politicians argued that the Church had overstepped its bounds. In 1984, for example, *The Washington Post* ran the following piece discussing the relationship between the Church and the political system on the abortion issue:

Cardinal Bernardin Urges Rejection of 'Single-Issue Politics'
Influential Catholic Leader Rebuts Stands Taken by Some Bishops on Abortion, Nuclear Arms

. . .Bernardin's speech comes in the midst of one of the fiercest debates in recent history on the relationship between religion and politics, a debate that has polarized American Catholics. Both Democratic vice-presidential nominee Geraldine Ferraro and New York Gov. Mario Cuomo have been criticized by Archbishop John O'Connor of New York, for not actively campaigning against abortion, and others in the Church hierarchy have urged Catholics to make abortion the primary issue in the November election.

Bernardin's role in spearheading the development of the American bishops' controversial pastoral letter condemning nuclear warfare and his leadership of the powerful Prolife Activities Committee of the National Conference of Catholic Bishops gives him a position of influence among Catholics in America. . . .

While condemning single issue politics, the cardinal defended the right of religious groups to join in political debate. "The First Amendment guarantees religious institutions the right to be heard in the public debate," he said.

At the same time, Bernardin distanced the Catholic Church from what he called "the religious right," because the latter "at times fails to address the complexity of our policy agenda and the legitimate secular quality of our popular discourse." . . . (10/26/84)

Four other divisive topics also received enough attention to make it into the top twenty. They illustrate how media attention changes with the times on issues of longstanding social import that nonetheless rise and fall on the news agenda. These topics included economic issues, women's issues, clerical celibacy and homosexuality. Foremost among these were economic issues, which finished just one story short of the top ten.

A total of 82 stories addressed questions of economic fairness, poverty, homelessness, etc. Economic issues were most heavily discussed at the beginning and end of the study period. Early discussions focused on poverty relief, while stories in the 1980s dealt with broader concerns of economic fairness connected to the 1986 pastoral letter by the U.S. Conference of Bishops. Several articles pointed out an "either-or" situation many churches faced: Whether to make church repairs and renovations or direct the money to aid the poor became an increasingly public question in the Church.

There were 30 discussions of economic issues in the 1960s, which focused on the traditional concerns of Catholic charities to alleviate the strains of poverty. These stories often focused on experimental programs to provide services to poor children, or gifts at Christmas, or programs set up by churches to feed the hungry. During the 1970s discussion of economic concerns dropped by half, to only 15 stories. In the 1980s attention picked up, and economic issues appeared in 37 stories. This upturn in the 1980s can be traced to two concerns. First, the Church was criticized for its alleged failure to deal with homelessness. This was raised most pointedly by homeless advocates like Mitch Snyder in Washington and others who thought the Church was doing too little, too late. Second, the pastoral letter from the Conference of Bishops urged the Church to do more to encourage a fair distribution of wealth and an adequate standard of living for all people. The newspapers gave economic discussions the heaviest play; they figured in five percent of all articles printed in both the *Times* and the *Post*. Economic concerns were raised in only three percent of CBS broadcasts and two percent of the stories at *Time*.

The push for women in the priesthood and other issues connected to women in the Church accounted for 68 stories overall. These issues were almost never discussed in the 1960s, when only two stories appeared in the sample. During the following decade, however, the feminist movement and dissident theologians began making demands on the Church for greater equality and recognition of women. Thus, the coverage leaped to 39 stories in the 1970s sample, before dropping back to 27 stories in the 1980s.

A *Washington Post* report on a Women's Ordination Conference sums up the tone of the changing coverage:

Catholic Women's Move
for Reform Goes Beyond Ordination
By Marjorie Hyer

At 6 a.m. Friday, on her tenth wedding anniversary, Denise Mantell, 32, kissed her husband and two children goodbye and left their

Queens, N.Y., home to spend the weekend here seeking ways to further her ambition to be a Roman Catholic priest.

Rina Pino-Vargas, 29, cradling her 4-month-old daughter Margarita in her arms, drove from Albuquerque, N.M., with a carload of other Hispanic Catholic women for the same purpose.

The two young mothers are typical of a movement that is coalescing to batter a 2,000-year-old barrier to priestly ordination of women in the Catholic Church.

More than 2,000 supporters of the cause — nuns, lay women and a handful of priests and lay men — gathered here over the weekend to plan strategy.

At one level the conference proceeded along the lines of the first such Women's Ordination Conference held in Detroit three years ago as participants explored the politics of ordaining women into the present church system. . . .(11/13/78)

Clerical celibacy was a point of debate in 41 stories in the sample. Most of these (26 stories) appeared in the 1960s, when there was a significant amount of internal dissent over the Church's insistence on celibacy. *The New York Times* quoted a Jesuit scholar who foresaw the end of clerical celibacy.

Jesuit Predicts End of Marriage Ban for Priests
By Edward B. Fiske

The Roman Catholic Church will be forced to change its rules that priests cannot marry "within five or six years," according to the Rev. Joseph H. Fichter, a prominent Jesuit sociologist.

"The change will be gradual and will begin with small steps — like readmitting priests who are already married," he said.

"But there is a growing consensus in the church that the celibacy requirement is unjust, and I'd say it has to and will be changed."

Father Fichter, a member of the Harvard University faculty, made his prediction during a three day symposium here on "Clerical Celibacy: An Option in the Priesthood?"

The conference — the first of its kind in this country — was sponsored by the National Association for Pastoral Renewal, an organization of about 900 American priests that seeks elimination of mandatory celibacy and other reforms in the Catholic priesthood. . . .

The Rev. Thomas Pucelik, 34, a theologian at Catholic University in Washington, who is the new president of the association, declared: "When I became a priest I didn't take on superhuman status. I took on a function — that of serving people in the name of God."

Father Pucelik said that this shift in the image of the priest explains the almost total rejection among conference delegates of Pope Paul VI's thinking in last June's encyclical "Sacerdotalis Caelibatus" ("On Priestly Celibacy"). It declared that celibacy would "continue to be firmly linked to the ecclesiastical ministry."

In arguing for optional celibacy, participants in the symposium nevertheless agreed unanimously that celibacy must continue to be regarded as a spiritual ideal for many. . . . (9/10/67)

Attention waned over the years, as celibacy was the topic of 11 stories in the 1970s sample before declining to only four stories in the 1980s. Dire predictions made in the 1960s that celibacy would drive the priesthood to extinction failed to come true, and many of the dissenters left the priesthood for other callings.

While celibacy faded as an issue, homosexuality went from no coverage in the 1960s to 9 stories in the 1970s and then to more than twice that number (21) in the 1980s. The following article from *Time* lays out the theological debate over homosexuality as the media reported it.

Sexual Dissent

Homosexual acts are intrinsically disordered and can in no way be approved of. (Vatican Declaration on Sexual Ethics, January 1976)

When the Congregation for the Doctrine of the Faith issued its 5,000 word statement on homosexuality, premarital sex and masturbation, it was responding in part to complaints that the church was not providing sufficient guidelines for sexual behavior and attitudes. Days later, Father John McNeill, a Jesuit priest and former teacher of moral theology at the now defunct Woodstock College and at Fordham University, won the designation "Imprimi Potest" ("It Can be Printed") for a book strongly attacking the church's views on homosexuality. It had taken two years to win that designation, which is not an endorsement. Jesuit Superior General Pedro Arrupe had delayed publication while McNeill consulted scholars and revised the book to specify ways in which it differs from church teachings.

One Night Stands. In the newly released book *The Church and the Homosexual* (Sheed Andrews and McMeel), McNeill finds those teachings an intolerable burden. The Catholic Church advocates that a homosexual should try to become a heterosexual and, if he fails, insists that he abstain from sex entirely because no homosexual act can be justified morally. McNeill maintains that such teaching results in "one-night stands" and "suffering, guilt and mental disorder." Instead, McNeill thinks the church should encourage "a mature homosexual relationship with one partner with the intention of fidelity," though he does not call this marriage. . . . (9/20/76)

This coincides with increased activism by gay Catholic groups like Dignity, which prompted debate over Church ministry to gays and lesbians. The 1980s added the AIDS crisis to the debate and Church response to these new needs often came under fire from activists.

How accurately does this issue agenda match the internal concerns of the Church? Of course, any judgment on the appropriateness of the media's issue agenda is necessarily subjective. But we can at least compare the coverage of the secular media with the judgments of journalists representing the Catholic press, to determine whether a different pattern of coverage might result from an insider's perspective. Each year the Catholic News Service polls editors at some of the largest Catholic publications in the United States and Canada to list the top ten issues of that year. From this list we compiled the top ten issues the editors chose during each time period in our study. The comparisons, which appear in Table 5 (p. 124), show considerable similarity early on, but increasing diversity in later years.

In the 1960s the Catholic editors agreed with the

secular media's actual coverage on eight out of ten topics, although the order of prominence differed. Our sample of secular media included more attention to education and economic issues than the editors' picks. The editors, on the other hand, gave greater emphasis to peace efforts (particularly those undertaken by the Pope) and clerical celibacy. Otherwise the two lists were very similar, with only slight differences in the order of some issues.

During the 1970s the agreement between the two lists dropped as diversity in the editors' picks increased. Both secular and Catholic media reflected an increasing number of issues confronting the Church, but Catholic editors identified more issues as significant over the five-year period. This time the two lists placed seven of the same issues in the top ten. Secular media gave greater attention to news about the Pope, ecumenical efforts and crimes by clerics from around the country. Secular attention to the Pope revolved around the personality profile pieces common for any celebrity. The Catholic editors gave little attention to the Pope as a celebrity, but emphasized Catholic hunger relief efforts, Church policies regarding divorce, and Church opposition to euthanasia.

By the 1980s, the two sets of news judgments diverged even more, and the two lists contained only six issues in common. Secular media outlets included education, women's issues, homosexuality, and Church happenings among the top ten issues that they covered. Catholic editors ignored those areas and added hunger relief efforts (for a second decade), changes in Church regulations, agricultural policies (particularly concerning family farmers), and the financial burdens placed on the Church by the retirement of many members of religious orders. They also assigned a higher priority to the Church's role in secular politics, ranking it as their number one concern, at a time when it ranked only eighth in national media coverage.

Sources

THE TOPICS OF discussion sketch out the broad agenda of issues that were dealt with in the media. The next question we asked is who supplied the information for these stories. To ascertain the origin of this information, we identified every source in every story who provided information or commentary for the news. This resulted in 5,644 identifiable source references. Of these, 70 percent (or 3,978 mentions) were individuals affiliated with the Church in one capacity or another (see table 6, p. 125).

The Church voices were dominated by the hierarchy, whose members were cited 2,201 times, accounting for over half (55 percent) of all Catholic sources. As defined here, the hierarchy included all members of the clergy at or above the level of bishop. Papal statements were responsible for 17 percent of these source citations, 364 in all. Priests and other members of religious orders trailed at a distant second with 810 mentions. These officials at the pastoral level accounted for 20 percent of all Catholic source citations. Lay Catholics were third with 510 citations (13 percent of Catholic sources). Officials and faculty members at Catholic schools and universities added 305 citations, or eight percent. Catholic publications, both national and local, comprised three percent of Catholic sources with 109 citations. Prominent dissidents like Hans Küng and Charles Curran added another one percent with 43 mentions.

Non-Catholic sources were led by the leaders of other churches. They were cited 297 times, most often reacting to new Vatican policies. These other religious voices accounted for 18 percent of the non-Catholic sources. Following close behind were officials of the United States government, who were used as sources 205 times to comprise one in eight non-Catholic sources (12 percent). Officials of state or local governments accounted for an additional eight percent of sources with 140 references. Foreign governments accounted for another 46 source citations in the news, or three percent of all non-Catholic sources. Abortion rights groups accounted for two percent of non-Catholic sources with 28 citations.

In addition to these general groups of sources we also looked at the prominence of particular individuals in the news (see table 7, p. 126). There were few differences in the distribution of sources by the various outlets in our study (see table 8, p. 127).

All outlets gave greatest play to members of the Church hierarchy for their statements. Interestingly, CBS ran the greatest number of statements from John Paul II. CBS quoted him 41 times, while *The Washington Post* cited him on 33 occasions. *The New York Times* trailed with 19 mentions, and *Time* came in last with 14 references. It appears that the Pope most comfortable with television was also popular on that medium. CBS quoted the fewest officials and faculty members from Catholic schools (14 citations or half the rate found at other outlets). This was probably a function of the few stories that the network did on the Catholic education system. CBS also relied on federal government officials for quotes more often than other outlets. Federal officials accounted for ten percent of sources on CBS, but no more than three percent at any other outlet.

Time differed from the others when it came to quotations from prominent Catholic dissidents. Two percent of all sources in *Time* were citations of Hans Küng and Father Curran, more than double the proportion at all the other outlets. In fact, this weekly magazine published more statements by dissidents than did any of the daily outlets. *Time's* attention to dissidents will reappear in our study as we examine the level of disagreement reported in stories. *The New York Times* stood out for its use of officials from state and local governments as sources. The *Times* printed the greatest number of statements from this group in absolute terms, and proportionately twice as many as any other outlet.

Presenting Church Teachings

A CENTRAL FOCUS of this inquiry is the presentation of opinions in the debate over issues involving the Church and its teachings. Before dealing with the particulars of this multifaceted debate, however, we sought to specify its overall parameters. First, how often are the Church's teachings presented in the news? Second, in what manner are they usually presented? Are they simply reported without debate, or are they challenged or refuted by critics or opponents? The answers to these questions provide the context for the issue debates that are recounted in the following sections.

Rather than make our own decisions about what constituted Church teaching, we only coded statements explicitly identified as representing the Church view. Once this was noted, we examined the rest of the story to see if any other source in the story argued against the Church teaching. This allowed us to differentiate between stories that merely recounted a Vatican statement from those that provided a broader context by including criticism of the doctrine. Obviously, a story that recounts the Church doctrine without debate has a quite different tone from one in which the Church has to respond to dissenting voices.

The Catholic Church has been fairly successful over the years in placing its official teachings in the news. Of the stories in our sample, 41 percent (763 stories) presented and specifically identified official doctrines of the Church. For example, in 1974 *The New York Times* quoted the Pope reiterating Church opposition to abortion, "The Church upholds man's inalienable right to live from the first beginning of his existence — a right that no human being can ever dispose of." (2/28/74) Another *Times* article simply stated Church policy, "Church law does not permit women to serve [as non-ordained ministers]." (10/31/87)

An additional 34 percent gave voice to Catholic clergy. Most often these individuals were presenting the teachings of the Church without making a specific claim to speak for the Church. For instance, Cardinal Bernardin would also comment on abortion, "Science cannot establish when the soul is infused in the fetus and human personhood begins. But it is because we do not know precisely when this happens that the life process at all stages of prenatal development must be protected. We must treat the fetus as a human person from the moment of conception or risk the taking of human life." (*The New York Times* 9/28/84)

A much smaller number of statements were provided by dissidents who voiced their discontent or opposition to Church policies or actions. The remaining stories simply covered an event without expressing the views of any group or presented the reactions of other churches to Catholic actions.

As was evident from the discussion of sources above, the hierarchy was a major voice in news of the Church. When we examine the orientation of stories over time, we find a similar pattern (see table 9, p. 127).

In addition, numerous stories quoted members of the clergy without identifying their views with those of the Church. When we examined the stories where the stated positions of clergy were not debated, we found that they were almost always reiterating Church teaching. In almost two-thirds of these stories (65 percent) there was no debate over these teachings. Adding together the stories that explicitly identified the Church's teaching with those in which clergy implicitly stated its teaching, a majority of all stories presented the Church's views on some issue, either with or without debate.

The increasing attention paid to the statements of individual clergy who did not identify their position as that of the Church does not reflect more attention paid to dissidents. It appears that more American bishops and cardinals were making statements to the media on various issues facing the American Church without explicitly speaking for the Church. For example, a pastoral letter from New York bishops restated the Church teaching on abortion, "Since laws which allow abortion violate the unborn child's God-given right, we are opposed to any proposal to extend them." (*The New York Times* 2/13/68)

The result is a picture of news that gave prominent position to the teachings of the Church. Even as disputes over difficult issues and disciplinary actions against dissidents received greater attention, the Church teaching was not shunted aside. There is, however, more to establishing the framework of the issue debate than the prominence of Church teachings. It is also necessary to know how many of these stories included some debate of these teachings. This provides a measure of the number of stories that had a confrontational tone in their presentation of the Church.

Therefore, we examined every story to identify those in which one or more Church teachings were criticized or rejected. Of the 763 stories that presented an official Church doctrine, half did so without debate (see table 10, p. 128). This reflects a tendency simply to reprint Church announcements without additional reporting. In the remaining stories that discussed Church policy, conflict was supplied by internal dissent, debates with other religions, and clashes with secular forces. Dissenters within the Church constituted the greatest single source of conflict. Thirty-nine percent of stories that identified Church stands also featured dissenting voices from laypersons or clergy.

As we shall discuss later, Church teachings on sexual morality and the distribution of authority within the Church were the major areas of internal conflict. For example, a 1985 *Time* article contained sharp criticism from several nuns on the status of women in the Church: " 'The Pope doesn't understand American women. This is our church, and we are not going to let a few men who work in the Vatican make it un-Christian.'. . . 'There was a time when the Church sanctioned slavery and burned heretics, and the patriarchal Church still does not see that there is anything to be sorry for in its treatment of women.'. . . 'The bishops are all hunkering down in the grass like a bunch of guinea hens. Wait a minute, I don't want to insult the hens. They don't stir a feather because they fear for their own tails.' " (*Time* 2/4/85)

Debates with other religions or secular authorities appeared in another 11 percent of stories. Arguments with other religions were most often connected to ecumenical efforts. Catholic-Jewish ties were frequently tense over issues like the Church's response to the Holocaust and the Pope's 1986 audience with Kurt Waldheim. Debates with political authorities occurred over such issues as public funding of private schools, the prosecution of clergymen for crimes, and efforts to legalize abortion.

This overall picture, however, masks significant differences among media outlets (see table 11, p. 128). *Time* magazine stood out as most likely to open Church views up to debate in its coverage, presenting the greatest proportion of conflict found in any of the outlets studied. Fewer than one-third (31 percent) of *Time's* stories presented Church teachings without debate. The two newspapers each presented Church teachings in almost equal proportions of contested and uncontested stories; 48 percent of stories in the *Post* and 51 percent of those in the *Times* presented Church teachings without debate. CBS presented the fewest stories with debate. Only one in four stories on TV featured any dissent or criticism of the Church's teaching.

There was also a marked change in the pattern of debate over the years (see table 12, p. 128). The sharpest change came in the 1980s, as an increasingly controversial slate of issues demanded Church attention. In the earlier time periods, a majority of stories presented Church teachings without debate. In the 1980s, that changed sharply, as nearly three stories in five (58 percent) debated Church doctrines.

This shift mainly reflected an increase in the number of stories presenting conflict with either a government agency or another religion. The amount of debate accounted for by internal dissent actually dropped from 45 percent of stories in the 1960s to 37 percent in the 1980s. Meanwhile, conflicts with outside groups rose from four percent of stories in the 1960s to 22 percent of stories in the 1980s. There were increasing debates over the Church's involvement in the American political scene over issues like abortion, diplomatic relations with the Vatican, and public funding for private schools. Additional tensions with Jews and Protestant sects raised criticism from other religious groups.

Introduction to Viewpoints

OVER THE YEARS since Vatican II, news coverage of the Catholic Church has developed a more confrontational tone, as stories came to include more debate on Church teachings from dissidents within and critics without. At the same time, Church teachings continued to be reported, and the hierarchy was always well represented in the debate. Thus, the battle of ideas involving the Church cannot be assessed fully from the distribution of topics and sources or the structure of stories involving Church teachings. It is necessary to examine directly how the news media presented the entire range of opinions on Church teachings and activities.

In order to understand how the policies and teachings of the Catholic Church were viewed in the media, we analyzed all opinions by sources or reporters on 36 different issues related to Church life. These included such frequently and heatedly debated topics as the status and role of women and minorities in the Church, the role of the laity, prohibitions of abortion, contraception and homosexual acts, debates over freedom of expression versus Church authority, Church-state relations, and ecumenism.

That an opinion be coded, the source or reporter had to make a clear appraisal of Church policy, stating agreement or disagreement with Church teachings. Ambiguous or unclear statements were not coded. Presenting the data separately on each of these 36 issues would be tedious and confusing, since many were addressed infrequently. Instead, we will present more general trends and examine views on particular issues only when they are noteworthy.

Most opinions clustered around four general areas of conflict. The most frequently discussed dimension dealt with Church stands on matters of sexual morality. This included opinions on five issue areas: prohibitions of abortion and artificial birth control, clerical celibacy, Church opposition to homosexual activity, and the moral and ethical problems posed by artificial reproductive technologies.

A second dimension concerned power relations within the Church. This consisted of opinions on the following issues: The status and role of women (including their ordination), the status and role of minorities, the proper role for the laity, questions of academic freedom at Catholic institutions, changes in the Mass and other liturgical reforms, and appraisals of how the Church has handled dissenters.

A third dimension was constructed to deal with power relations between the Church and State authority. This included opinions in four distinct areas: Questions of public funding for private schools, Church involvement in politics, Church teachings and policies regarding war, and the broader question of the proper separation of church and state.

The fourth and final dimension dealt with ecumenism and relations among churches. This dimension included opinions on the desirability of Christian unity, obstacles to Christian unity, Catholic-Jewish relations, and relations between the Church and other faiths, especially the various Protestant denominations.

The largest group of opinions concerned matters of sexual morality (see table 13, p. 128). There were 249 opinions judging Church teachings on sexual matters, accounting for 30 percent of all opinions on Church policy found in the news. The patterns of power and authority in the Church were the next most frequently discussed dimension. There were 185 opinions about this group of issues in our sample, representing 22 percent of all opinions coded. Discussions of ecumenism were next in frequency, comprising 105 opinions or 13 percent of the entire total. Bringing up the rear, with only 45 opinions, were discussions of church-state relations. This set of issues accounted for only five percent of all opinions identified.

The most frequent subject of debate concerned Church teachings on sexual morality. *Time* was the outlet most preoccupied with this cluster of issues. Forty-two percent of all viewpoints found in the magazine dealt with sexual issues. *The New York Times* was next, with 36 percent of all viewpoints discussing issues of sexual morality. At CBS, 25 percent of all opinions dealt with sexual morality. *The Washington Post* finished last, with 22 percent of all opinions discussing sexual matters.

The *Post* focused instead on power relations, a topic on which it was the clear leader in coverage. Power relations in the Church accounted for 30 percent of all viewpoints found in the *Post*. This is nearly twice the rate of its nearest competitor, *Time*, where 19 percent of all viewpoints dealt with power structures. At both CBS and *The New York Times*, 16 percent of all viewpoints dealt with power relations.

Ecumenism and relations between churches received relatively little attention at any outlet. Fourteen percent of all *The Washington Post* opinions dealt with ecumenism, followed by CBS, with 11 percent. *Time* and *The New York Times* each dealt with ecumenism in nine percent of the viewpoints they published.

All four outlets devoted even less attention to church-state relations. Indeed, *Time* virtually ignored this topic, running only three statements of opinion, or two percent of its opinion coverage. But coverage was not much heavier at the other outlets. Church-state relations accounted for six percent of all opinions in the *Post* and seven percent in the *Times*, rising to a maximum of eight percent of opinions aired on CBS.

Sexual Morality
Roman Catholics
The Anger of a Rebel

. . . As a result of the church's puritanical approach to moral issues, says Rev. James Kavanaugh, "the Catholic is obsessed with sex" — as he, for one, seems to be. About three fourths of his examples of Church-imposed agony involve sex; most of the cases are described in prose that might seem a trifle fetid for a true confession magazine. At Catholic girls' colleges, he says, "to French kiss or not to French kiss is usually the question. Keeping the teeth closed becomes the ancient badge of the martyrs who refused to sacrifice to the pagan gods of Rome. She firms her lips and guards her tongue with all the ardor of a convent under siege."

Restricted and Impoverished. Illustrating the problems created by the Church's ban on divorce, he tells of the suffering Catholic whose wife flaunted her infidelity by coming home with other men. "He heard her laugh on the sofa downstairs, heard her moans of pleasure. Finally, he left her. He met another girl who made him know he was a man. He came to his priest and learned that one burst of semen had bound him to a whore." (*Time* 7/7/67)

The national media do not always take such a voyeuristic interest in sexual issues. Nonetheless, this topic added a certain spice to the religion beat that did not go unnoticed by reporters and editors. Sexual mores were at issue in many cases of dissent (as they were for Father Kavanaugh). Church teachings on sexual practices were often seen as an impediment to ecumenism, and in some cases they put Church policy in conflict with government policy. All this combined to make discussions of sex and the Catholic Church the leading topic of controversy in every time period and almost every outlet in the study. The only exception was *The Washington Post*, perhaps the nation's most politically oriented newspaper. At the *Post*, appropriately enough, the debate over sexual morals took second place to discussions of power relations within the Church.

This dimension included the controversial areas of Church teachings on abortion, birth control, artificial reproductive technologies, priestly celibacy and homosexuality. We will first examine the balance of opinion that directly expressed support or criticism of Church teachings, excluding general statements on these controversial issues that did not address the Church's teaching. This narrow definition of the issue debate provides the clearest measure of opinion for and against the Church. One could argue, however, that all opinions on abortion, birth control, etc. in news stories dealing with the Church are relevant to the Church's portrayal, even when they do not specifically address the Church's doctrines. Therefore, we analyzed this broader set of opinions as well.

Among all statements that clearly expressed their agreement or disagreement with Church teachings on these issues, about four out of seven (56 percent) disagreed with the Church. However, this level of disagreement was not consistent across outlets, sources, time periods, or particular issues.

Differences in the balance of opinion at the various media outlets proved noteworthy (see table 14, p. 129). The Church received its greatest support on CBS broadcasts, where more than two out of three sources (69 percent) agreed with Church teachings on sex. At *The New York Times*, the proportions were exactly the opposite of the overall figures, with 56 percent of opinions supporting the Church. However, the preponderance of support for Church teachings at these outlets was outweighed by opposition at the other two. In the pages of *The Washington Post*, fewer than one third of all opinions (32 percent) expressed agreement with the Church. At *Time*, 38 percent of sources agreed with Church teachings.

Even more striking was the opinion breakdown among

different types of sources (see table 15, p. 129). Church teachings on sexual morality were endorsed almost exclusively by members of the hierarchy. Nearly nine out of ten statements (88 percent) from clergy at the level of bishop or above supported the Church's teachings. Priests and members of religious orders below the level of bishop were even more unified on the opposite side — 91 percent of their quotes opposed Church teachings. Members of the laity and non-Catholics were also overwhelmingly opposed (86 and 85 percent opposition respectively). The overall effect was to present the debate over sexual morality as a split between the Church hierarchy and everyone else. Nonetheless, agreement with Church teachings on these matters actually rose over time (see table 16, p. 130). In the 1960s, only 36 percent of sources agreed with Church teachings. By the 1970s that proportion had risen to 56 percent, before dropping slightly to 52 percent during the 1980s. The reasons for the differences between outlets and over time can be found in the differing levels of attention given to specific issues, as well as shifts in the distribution of sources who provided comment.

The most frequently discussed area of moral teaching was the Church ban on artificial methods of birth control, which yielded 124 opinions. A distant second was taken by debates over priestly celibacy, which generated 70 statements pro and con. Trailing far behind was the abortion issue, which prompted only 34 direct appraisals of the Church's opposition. Catholic opposition to homosexual behavior accounted for 15 opinions, while the controversy over artificial reproductive technologies generated only six comments.

Not only did these specific issues receive different amounts of attention, there were also significant differences in the balance of opinion from one issue to another (see table 17, p. 130). On the issues of abortion, homosexuality, and artificial reproduction, sources who directly assessed Church teaching usually supported those teachings. For example, 56 percent of sources agreed with the Church's condemnation of abortion. Two thirds of the sources who discussed the Church opposition to homosexual acts agreed with its teaching. The same level of support was found for Church opposition to artificial reproductive technologies, although few opinions were expressed.

The areas marked by the greatest criticism were requirements of priestly celibacy and the Church's denunciation of the use of artificial methods of birth control. These were also the issues that attracted by far the heaviest reporting of opinions on this dimension. When questioned on the issue of celibacy, 73 percent of sources rejected the Church doctrine. The condemnation of the use of artificial contraception attracted more debate, but the distribution of opinion was also more balanced. When discussing Catholic teaching on birth control, 53 percent of sources disagreed with the Church doctrine that artificial contraception was wrong.

Most of the shift of opinion on this dimension can be explained by changing reactions to the Church stand on birth control. In the 1960s, the publication of *Humanae Vitae* prompted 84 statements on this newly reiterated teaching. This period accounts for two thirds of all the debate on birth control found in the study. During this era, sources disagreed with Church teaching on artificial contraception by more than a three-to-two margin (61 vs. 39 percent).

Criticism of the encyclical came from all quarters, with most critiques originating within the Church. One of the most frequently quoted criticisms came from a group of

Catholic theologians who argued, "spouses may responsibly decide according to their conscience that artificial contraception in some circumstances is permissible and indeed necessary to preserve and foster the values and sacredness of marriage." (*The New York Times* 8/1/68) A group of Minneapolis priests were even more critical: ". . . obedience to Pope Paul's encyclical banning birth control may result in exactly the things the ban was aimed to prevent — infidelity and loss of respect." (*The Washington Post* 8/10/68) Criticism from outside the Church was sharply summarized by the independent Roman newspaper, *Il Messaggero*: "The problems that the world faces under population pressures cannot be entrusted to the intelligence of single men, nor to the calculations of natural rhythms regarding the reproductive system." (*The Washington Post* 7/31/68)

Defenders of *Humanae Vitae*, who were usually representatives of the Church hierarchy, were every bit as clear in their support for the doctrine. Cardinal McIntyre called the encyclical: ". . . refreshing in an age grown confused by the changing and subjective theories of situational ethics and morality." (*The Washington Post* 7/30/68) The Vatican's official news organ, *L'Osservatore Romano*, was more emphatic: "[artificial contraception] is a mental, moral and physical mutilation." (*The Washington Post* 7/31/68)

By the 1970s, however, the margin of opinion had shifted in favor of the Church. At the same time, the number of sources debating the issue dropped to less than one quarter of its previous level. In the 1970s, only 20 sources debated the Church ban on artificial contraception. A *Time* magazine article from 1976 cited a poll showing opposition to Church teachings: "In 1968, Pope Paul VI issued his encyclical *Humanae Vitae*, explicitly telling Catholics they were forbidden to use artificial methods of contraception. In 1974, a study of American Catholics showed that fully 83 percent did not accept such teaching." To drive home this point, the story went on to quote a Catholic mother of three who said, "If my daughter wants to lead an active sex life, I consider it a moral obligation to give her all the information I can on birth control." (5/24/76)

These two quotes illustrate much of the waning debate in the media over prohibitions on birth control. As more and more polls indicated that American Catholics were not following the teaching, the subject was relegated to debate within the Church and no longer raised much concern from external critics. It had been these external criticisms that swung the balance of media-borne opinion against the Church during the 1960s.

In the 1980s, the margin of opinion widened to almost two-to-one in favor of the Church teaching on birth control (65 vs. 35 percent). The amount of debate remained equal to 1970s levels, with 20 statements pro and con. The further shift of opinion in the Church's favor was largely due to the internal nature of the discussions, in which the Catholic hierarchy provided the dominant voices.

The birth control debate illustrates how the participants (i.e. the choice of sources) have a great deal to do with the balance of views printed and broadcast (see table 18, p. 130). In the debate over the ban on artificial contraception, a large group of secular sources slowly faded from view over time, leaving the debate to groups within the Church. In the 1960s, the publication of *Humanae Vitae* brought a flood of criticism from secular forces basing themselves on world hunger and an exploding world population. At one international conference after another, leaders urged plans to limit population growth. In 1968 many saw the Pope's encyclical as a direct assault on the wisdom of their plans and were quick to voice their opposition.

This secular assault, combined with internal dissent, shifted the balance against the Church. Among all of the identified Catholic sources, opinion was 53 to 47 percent opposed to the Church. This narrow split, however, conceals the same fault line between laity and hierarchy that we found on this dimension of opinion overall. Members of the Church hierarchy above the level of priests made 39 statements on both sides of the issue, dominating the discussion. Of the 16 views expressed by laymen, 87 percent disagreed with the Church prohibition. The hierarchy, on the other hand, were 77 percent in favor of the Church teaching. Priests and other members of religious orders were less likely to support the Church than the laity with 93 percent disagreeing with the Church. Non-Catholic sources were unanimously opposed to the Church prohibition on artificial means of birth control.

In the 1970s, the media debate became almost totally intramural, as only one non-Catholic source expressed an opinion. The secular world (including the major media) had moved on to other problems, and opinion polls continued to show that large numbers of Catholics were ignoring the Church ban. In this new milieu, Church teachings were debated 19 times and affirmed 63 percent of the time. As in the 1960s, the laity who were quoted remained firmly opposed to the ban on artificial methods of birth control, by a margin of 86 to 14 percent. By contrast, the hierarchy had solidified its ranks, supporting Church teachings in 100 percent of the statements quoted. The one cleric identified from outside the hierarchy spoke against the Church. Without the extra criticism from secular sources, the hierarchy became the dominant voice on the birth control issue.

The 1980s saw even less internal dissent, and Church teachings were affirmed 65 percent of the time. The handful of lay comments were all opposed to the Church pronouncements, just as they had been earlier. Priests and other members of religious orders supported the Church in only 25 percent of opinions. Meanwhile, the leadership supported Church teachings in all statements. Pope John Paul II's decision to reaffirm these teachings was a significant source of support in the 1980s. Coverage and repetition of his pronouncements alone yielded 31 percent of the affirmations of Church doctrine.

The outlets we studied differed considerably in their balance of opinion on this issue. The Catholic stand on birth control was affirmed in all six opinions aired on CBS. (This was largely due to the network's reliance on Church sources for opinions on this issue.) At *The New York Times*, Church teachings on birth control were affirmed more than twice as often as they were rejected (68 vs. 32 percent). In the pages of *The Washington Post*, these proportions were reversed. Church prohibitions on artificial birth control were discussed 48 times in the *Post*, and nearly two out of three of these sources (65 to 35 percent) rejected Church teaching. Similarly, sources in *Time* magazine rejected Church bans on artificial birth control by almost a two-to-one margin (64 to 36 percent of the 39 opinions).

While debate over birth control teachings accounted for most of the changes on this dimension, celibacy was also a major topic of debate. Priestly celibacy was one of the few areas of contention on which opinions did not change much over time, possibly because it was presented entirely as an internal debate among priests and their superiors.

The 1960s were the period of greatest conflict over celibacy, as radical priests frequently expressed their views in the news media. A total of 40 opinions were expressed in the debate over celibacy in the 1960s. Opponents usually forecast dire consequences to the Church if it continued to insist on celibacy for its priests. One priest argued that the requirement of celibacy was ". . . tearing the priesthood apart and forcing the best priests to lead unreal lives." (*The New York Times* 6/11/67) Another dissident priest (on leave of absence to join the war on poverty) said, "I don't believe a man's fundamental human right to marry can ever be violated simply because he wants to be a priest." (*The Washington Post* 11/5/67)

Defenses of the Church were often more low-key and only rarely offered by anyone lower in the hierarchy than a bishop. In a notable exception to this pattern, *The New York Times* reported, "A conservative Roman Catholic polling organization . . . has released the results of a poll showing that 90.7 percent of pastors in New York state believe that to permit priests to marry would not be beneficial to the church." (11/23/67) (If this poll accurately represented pastoral opinion on this issue, it would challenge the validity of the media's overall portrayal of the celibacy debate, since most priests who were quoted questioned the Church teaching.) Most defenses simply reiterated the Church reasoning that celibacy followed the example set by Christ.

The 1970s saw discussion of celibacy drop off dramatically to 18 statements on both sides of the issue combined. Other issues dominated Church concerns, among them calls for the ordination of women and greater racial equality within the Church. Support for the Church teaching was no more spirited in the 1970s, as this lukewarm endorsement from a lay Catholic illustrates: "I cannot see how one could have children and be a full time priest. He would have to spend more time on his children's development and less on the parish problems." (*Time* 5/24/76) Even in the 1980s, with much less discussion, there were few supporting voices. *The New York Times* cited its own poll, which found that 63 percent of Catholics favored allowing priests to marry (8/24/86).

The abortion issue was one on which news organizations differed significantly in the amount of discussion presented (see table 19, p. 131). *The New York Times* published 15 statements on both sides of the debate. *The Washington Post* and CBS, in contrast, each presented only five opinions on Church teaching regarding abortion. *Time* magazine ran nine arguments over Church theology on abortion, nearly double the number appearing in the *Post*, despite publishing only weekly editions.

The outlets also differed in the balance of opinion they presented on the abortion issue. Overall opinion on abortion broke 56 percent in support of the Church. At CBS and *The New York Times* sources were squarely behind the Church teachings. At CBS the margin was three-to-two (60 to 40 percent), while at the *Times* the split was nearly three-to-one (73 vs. 27 percent) in support of the Church. The *Times* printed two powerful statements by Pope Paul VI providing the reasons for the Church opposition to abortion: "Every crime against life is a blow to peace especially if it strikes at the moral conduct of the people . . . with horrible and often legal ease, as in the case of the suppression of incipient life, by abortion."(12/15/76) "What drug, what legal gilding can ever deaden the remorse of a woman who has freely and consciously murdered the fruit of her womb?" (1/2/77)

By contrast, sources in the pages of *The Washington Post* broke out three to two against the Church stand on abortion. A *Post* article quoted a full page ad in *The New York Times* signed by several Catholics calling for ". . . candid and respectful discussion of the abortion issue, challenging the church's teaching that abortion is always morally wrong." (12/19/84) The same *Post* article also gave space to the Church response, "Archbishop Quinn said the ad, 'contradicts the clear and constant teaching of the church that abortion is objectively immoral; it is not a legitimate choice.' "

In *Time* the Church condemnation of abortion was rejected twice as often as it was affirmed. For example, an Episcopal priest argued: ". . . the contention that the fetus, being viable, is to be regarded as a human being is not only specious, but begs the consideration that the sperm is also viable. Not even the most austere Catholic moralist suggests that the loss of semen through nocturnal emission is the taking of a life." (*Time* 2/10/67)

Over the course of time, positions on the Church's opposition to abortion shifted in unexpected ways. The changes resulted from the way the Church's teaching was presented as one component of the broader debate over abortion rights in American society and politics. In the 1960s, there were eight statements evenly divided between the two camps. During the 1970s there were nine statements on the Church condemnation of abortion, of which seven supported the Church. This was due to the reiteration of the Catholic doctrine by members of the hierarchy in response to the *Roe v. Wade* decision. By the 1980s, the amount of debate had nearly doubled, to 17 statements. Opinion was now slightly opposed to the Church. This can largely be attributed to secular groups stepping up their campaign for abortion rights and to a group of dissenting nuns and priests who made headlines with a *New York Times* ad requesting a change in Church policy. This prompted the Church to reassert its traditional teaching more frequently.

In contrast to the shifting currents of abortion coverage, all outlets except *The Washington Post* ran a majority of statements affirming Catholic teachings on homosexuality.

At the *Post*, opinion was evenly divided between support and criticism. Overall there were only 15 statements on the Church teachings against homosexual behavior. CBS aired only one statement of opinion, which supported the Church. *The New York Times* printed three statements that were also unanimous in their support of the Church. *The Washington Post* provided the most discussion with eight statements, which were evenly split on the issue. *Time* carried three statements, which split two to one in favor of the Church. At the four outlets combined, 67 percent of all opinion supported the Church doctrine.

No debate over the Church's doctrine on homosexuality appeared during the 1960s in our sample. In the 1970s, four out of the five opinions printed supported Church opposition to homosexuality. During the 1980s the frequency of opinion doubled, and the ten statements that appeared split six to four in support of the Church. Much of the increase in discussion of homosexuality came in connection to Church responses to the AIDS crisis and the tactics of gay rights groups like ACT UP. For example, *The Washington Post* quoted a director of Dignity criticizing the Pope for his response to AIDS, "If offering God's love is all he has to say about it, it is shocking. If that is all he has to say on AIDS, he has done the Church and gays a real disservice." (9/18/87)

The Church had a good bit more to say on homosexuality. When New York City passed an ordinance banning discrimination against homosexuals in city contracts, Cardinal O'Connor objected, "We would rather close our childcare agencies than violate Church teaching." (*The Washington Post* 6/20/84) On his visit to the U.S. a few years later Pope John Paul told bishops, ". . . homosexuals should practice 'chastity' if they want to be good Catholics." (*The Washington Post* 9 / 18 / 87)

Despite the host of ethical, legal and technical considerations they involve, artificial reproductive technologies (surrogate motherhood, in vitro fertilization, etc.), generated only six statements of opinion, all in the 1980s. Four of the six supported the Church. We encountered no viewpoints from *The Washington Post* on the subject. CBS aired one supportive comment. *Time* printed one statement for and one against the Church teaching on these technologies. *The New York Times* featured two supporters of the Church and one critic.

We have so far confined our analysis to opinions that directly affirmed or denied Church teaching on these five areas of sexual morality. To give a more complete picture of coverage, we also identified opinions regarding these areas that did not specifically address the Church's teachings. For example, we recorded abortion rights and anti-abortion opinions that did not directly express support or criticism of the Church. By including these more general statements regarding sexual morality in the analysis, we obtained a more complete portrait of the news context surrounding coverage of Church teachings.

When we examined this more inclusive dimension of moral issues, the number of opinions increased by nearly 50 percent (from 249 to 373), and all of the outlets moved closer to balanced views. Overall, opinion on this broader dimension was 54 percent opposed to or critical of positions taken by the Church, a slight drop from the 56 percent level of opposition found along the narrower dimension. Thus, the news was slightly more balanced on controversies involving sexual morality when the debate did not specifically reflect the teaching of the Catholic Church.

At CBS and *The New York Times*, support for Church teachings was still expressed by a slight majority of sources, but the proportion dropped to 52 percent. *The*

Washington Post had carried the most direct criticisms of the Church, but on this broader dimension criticism dropped ten percent, so that 58 percent of sources disagreed with Church moral teachings in these areas. *Time* magazine also continued to present more criticisms of Church teachings than defenses. On this broader dimension, 59 percent of sources quoted in *Time* disagreed with Church teachings.

Over the three time periods in the study, opinion was more varied on this broader dimension than it was among sources directly assessing Church doctrines. During the 1960s, Church teachings were supported by 37 percent of sources, virtually identical to the margin found on the narrower dimension. As with the narrower dimension, opinion swung sharply in support of Church teachings during the 1970s. Support for Church doctrines rose to 59 percent of sources, a slight increase over the narrower dimension. No single issue dominated support for the Church on this broader dimension. Instead, every issue discussed saw small increases in the amount of agreement with the Church's stands.

The 1980s, however, marked a downward trend in support for Church teachings not seen in the narrower dimension. Endorsements of positions shared by the Church were made by a minority of sources, representing 47 percent of opinions. This shift in the 1980s to increased criticism was due to debate over birth control and the acceptability of homosexuality. Defenders of homosexuality now outnumbered critics by five to four. More dramatic was the shift on birth control. Support for birth control remained at the same levels as in the 1970s, but sources opposing birth control almost disappeared from the news.

Power Relations in the Church

The news media gave heavy coverage to issues of power and authority in the Church, since conflicts of power in major institutions are treated as intrinsically newsworthy. The highly centralized, hierarchical structure of the Church has come under a great deal of criticism from both internal and external observers.

While all decisions, policies and teachings of the Church carry with them some notion of control and at least imply an exercise of authority, our definition of this dimension was much more limited. In this thematic dimension we were only concerned with issues that related to the institutional positions of power and authority within the Church. Thus, these became opinions about how the structure of the Church should or should not be recast to accommodate new groups.

To construct this thematic dimension we examined opinions on the following issues: the status of women in the Church, including the debate over ordaining women; the status of racial and ethnic minorities and their representation in the Church hierarchy; charges of racism in the Church; the proper role of the laity; academic freedom at Catholic educational institutions; and the handling of dissent within the Church.

Opinions in news stories consistently favored decentralizing power in the Church, usually by sharing it with groups that did not already have positions of authority. Support for change was almost twice as frequent as defense of the status quo, (64 vs. 36 percent of opinions). This strong support for changing the Church power structure undoubtedly grew from the changes enacted at Vatican II. Several resolutions expanded the role of bishops and cardinals as well as strengthening the position of local priests. Changes in the liturgy and structure of the Mass provided room for more lay involvement. Expansion in the numbers and stature of Eucharistic ministers and the Diaconate provided new opportunities for devout lay people.

In the 1960s, opinions on Church power structures favored change by almost a two-to-one margin, 66 to 34 percent (see table 20, p. 131). Many of these calls for change came from the Church itself, as it pushed reforms in many areas. The proportion of support for change remained steady in the 1970s. During this era the Church struggled to work out the details of the power-sharing outlined by the Second Vatican Council almost a decade earlier. By the 1980s, change lost some of its momentum, and there was a stronger defense of the status quo. The margin narrowed to 60 versus 40 percent in favor of a power shift. By this time, however, the hierarchy was not so frequently found on the side of change. This slight shift in opinion accompanied a rise in the number of sources debating power relations in the Church. There were 38 opinions either for or against changing the status quo reported in the 1960s. It did not become an area of extensive debate until after the conclusion of Vatican II and the task became sorting out the details of reform. By the 1970s the number of opinions had almost doubled to 71, a level that was maintained into the 1980s, when there were 75 opinions reported on one side or the other.

As we found in the debate over sexual morality, the views expressed largely followed from a source's relationship to the Church (see table 21, p. 131). Defenders of the status quo were concentrated among the hierarchy, who split two-to-one (65 to 35 percent) in favor of current patterns of authority. Once again the laity and most clergy below the level of bishop link up on the other side. Among these clergy, 78 percent of opinions quoted were opposed to the Church's exercise of authority, as were 69 percent of the statements by lay Catholics. Among non-Catholics opposition was almost unanimous, by 91 to nine percent.

Discussions of power structures within the Church were mainly the purview of *The Washington Post*. The *Post* printed 106 statements on both sides of the issue, more than the other three outlets combined. *The New York Times* was a distant second, printing 37 opinions. *Time* followed close behind with 32 opinions. CBS was last with only ten opinions about issues of power.

The Church's traditions came under attack with regard to both its treatment of constituent groups and its handling of dissent. As table 22 (p. 132) shows, most sources rejected the status quo with regard to the position of women, minorities, and the laity within the Church. Opinion was most balanced with regard to the role of women, with most of the debate revolving around proposals for the ordination of female priests. This was by far the most frequently debated issue on this dimension. By contrast, criticism of the Church's treatment of racial minorities was nearly unanimous, with 89 percent of sources either criticizing the Church as racist or calling for greater equality or representation for minorities. Similarly, nearly three out of four sources rejected the current role of the laity or argued for expanded influence by lay Catholics.

The Church fared just as poorly on issues of internal dissent (see table 23, p. 132). Two out of three sources condemned its handling of dissenters in its ranks, and three out of four criticized its response to issues involving freedom of expression (such as academic freedom at Catholic universities).

We turn now to the reasons behind the changes over time and the differences among outlets. As would be expected, one of the central factors to shifts in opinion on this dimension was institutional affiliation. There were clear distinctions between the hierarchy and the laity on these issues. Shifts in the relative numbers from these

Media Coverage of the Catholic Church

groups account for overall changes in opinion.

The only recurrent voices defending the status quo were those of the Church hierarchy. The hierarchy accounted for 62 percent of arguments for the status quo, while the laity added another 30 percent. Voices outside the Church made up the remaining eight percent. Not only was the hierarchy the most often heard, it was the only group to support the status quo. Nearly two thirds (65 percent) of the views expressed by the hierarchy favored the status quo. The laity favored change by an even greater margin, 69 to 31 percent. Priests and other officials at the pastoral level were even less likely to defend the status quo, at only 22 percent. Lay sources expressed support in 31 percent of statements.

The views of the hierarchy shifted over time to a more marked defense of the existing order, while lay opinion quoted in the media continued to support efforts for change. In the 1960s, the changes proposed by Vatican II, combined with the civil rights struggle in the Church, left the hierarchy ambivalent toward changing the status quo with a 50-50 split of opinion. Priests and other low-ranking clergy supported change in 69 percent of their statements. The laity followed suit to a slightly lesser degree, with a 64 to 36 percent margin favoring change. At this point in time the hierarchy was struggling against dissidents like the Catholic Traditionalist Movement, who did not want to abandon the Latin Mass or other rituals the Church had opted to change. Non-Catholic sources were unanimously for change.

By the 1970s, a major split had opened up between laity and hierarchy sources in the news. Lay support for change had increased to 85 percent of opinions, while the hierarchy defended the status quo almost as frequently — 83 percent of all opinions. Priests and other members of religious orders sided with the laity opting for change in Church structures in 87 percent of statements. At this point the Church was trying to rein in a movement that many thought was out of hand. For example, one woman explained that she wanted to change the structure of the Church ". . . from that of a male-dominated, transnational, religious corporation based in Rome, to that of a people's church, with a people's ministry, nurtured locally in parishes and base communities throughout the world. . ." (*The Washington Post* 11/13/78) The more traditionalist view of the Church was given by then Archbishop Bernardin, ". . . 'honesty and concern for the Catholic community' compelled him to speak on [women's ordination] so that Church leaders 'not seem to encourage unreasonable' hopes and expectations, even by their silence. Therefore, I am obliged to restate the Church's teaching that women are not to be ordained to the priesthood."

By the 1980s, the proportion of lay opinion favoring change had dropped to 59 percent. Widely announced Vatican drives for theological orthodoxy and a tightening of control by bishops tended to rein in some of the more divergent views on the structure of the Church. Priests and other clergy now advocated changing Church structures in 66 percent of statements. The hierarchy's views also shifted, now divided 52 to 48 percent on the issue of changing the status quo. This reflected a spread of opinions of a variety of issues, some meeting with Church approval while others were rejected by the Church leadership. Thus, solid majorities of lay opinion quoted always favored changing Church structures and procedures, while sources in the hierarchy switched sides over time.

These shifts of opinion accompanied changes in the focus of the debate. In the 1960s, almost half (45 percent) of opinions on power relations dealt with the laity. Proposed changes in the lay role and changes in the Mass accounted for 17 viewpoints. Issues of free expression (e.g., phasing out the Index of Books, dissent, etc.) accounted for another 16 opinions. In both of these areas where the Church was urging change, opinion favored changing the status quo by almost a two-to-one margin (64 to 36 percent).

Even in this period, when the Church seemed more tolerant of dissent, an unsigned *Time* article conjured up some sinister imagery to criticize the Vatican's former efforts against dissent, "In the early 20th century, the Roman Catholic Church had its own secret police. . . . Benigni's ecclesiastical SMERSH even had its own secret code and pseudonyms. . . . Some Church historians now contend that the repressive measures of Pius X (who was proclaimed a saint in 1954) stunted Catholic intellectual development for a generation. . . . Last week, Vatican sources reported, Pope Paul VI decided to abolish the oath taking requirement . . . in the future, priests will simply be required to make a general statement of support for the teachings of the Church." (7/28/67)

There were only five opinions during this period on such controversial issues as the ordination of women and racism in the Church. Three sources addressed minority concerns, and the remaining two addressed the ordination of women. Interestingly, a mild self-criticism of the Jesuits by Father Arrupe was the only foreshadowing of charges of racism to come, "The Society of Jesus has not committed the manpower and other resources . . . in any degree commensurate with the needs of the Negro to share in our services." (*The Washington Post* 11/11/67)

The ordination of women was demanded by a theology professor who concluded that the Church must "exorcise the demons of sexual prejudice by among other things admitting women to the priesthood." (*Time* 4/19/68) Cardinal Cushing spoke out against the ordination of women in 1964: "I could never confess my sins to a woman, it would be like doing it on television." (*Time* 8/24/64)

The 1970s saw a dramatic change in this arena of debate. Women's rights and status became the major point of contention, generating 47 opinions. The role and status of the laity were discussed by 15 sources, while issues of freedom of expression were discussed only five times. As racism and sexism became a larger point of debate, the Church often found itself under attack from a variety of secular sources. These larger issues could be connected to broader social ills. For instance, a mock pastoral letter from the National Organization for Women outlined the perceived failings of the Church in all of these areas: "Maternally, we admonish you to develop a self-critical ability with which to combat the blind idolatry of wealth, which has resulted in sexism, racism and classism within the Church. . ." (*The Washington Post* 4/25/77) The dramatic rise in discussion of women's issues highlights changes in the larger world that drew the Church into broader social controversies.

The most heavily reported issue of this period was the ordination of women to the priesthood, which alone generated 45 published opinions. These sources favored ordination by a 58 to 42 percent margin. The issue raised a great deal of internal dissent as well as criticism from feminist groups. For instance, the secretary of the Catholic Theological Society of America presented the group's opposition to the Church: "The bottom line is that there is no good reason not to ordain women." (*The Washington Post* 6/10/78) A missionary priest argued that if priests should resemble Christ and his disciples, "the priesthood should only be open to fishermen and Jews." (*Time* 2/7/77) And an elderly parishioner commented, "If a woman wants to be a priest, that's fine with me. The important thing is not who gives you Communion, but rather you believe it is sacrosanct." (*Time* 5/24/76)

For its part, the Church defended its ban on the ordination of women more sensitively than Cardinal Cushing had done ten years earlier. The justification was to be found in the examples of Christ according to a Vatican statement: "Jesus did not call any women to become part of the twelve. If he acted in this way, it was not in order to conform to the customs of his time, for his attitude toward women was quite different from that of his milieu . . . there would not be this 'natural resemblance' which must exist between Christ and his minister, if the role of Christ were not taken by a man. . . ." (*The Washington Post* 1/28/77) The status and rights of women were also found wanting on two occasions. One nun accused ". . . the male hierarchies of organized religions of oppressing women by treating them as a subordinate sex." (*The New York Times* 10/25/74)

Debate over issues concerning the laity remained at previous levels. However, opinion was now split 53 to 47 percent in favor of changing the status quo. A young woman voiced her support for change in *Time*: "When I was a kid, you didn't understand what was happening in Mass. You played with your rosary beads, which had nothing to do with anything. Now we aren't just sitting in Mass, we're participating." But another parishioner in the same article voiced her opposition: "I feel a little bit lost. I miss the time for silent prayer. Now you jump and sing. . ." (5/24/76)

Issues of freedom of expression were the least discussed. But all five opinions in the sample criticized Church handling or favored a more lenient approach to dissent and freedom of opinion. For instance, when a Jesuit priest was dismissed from his order after he baptized the child of a

Catholic who supported legalized abortion, he charged it was a "kangaroo court . . . I felt I was railroaded because I had been given no written charges. . ." (*The Washington Post* 9/7/74)

By the 1980s, the power and role of the laity had ceased to be an issue, garnering only two opinions. On the other hand, discussions of women's and minority rights continued at high levels. There were 46 opinions on this group of issues across all the outlets studied. Issues of academic freedom and freedom of opinion generated another 27 opinions.

Women's issues received slightly less attention than they had in the 1970s with 36 opinions, down from 45 statements in the previous decade. Debates on the status of women still found the Church lacking, by a two-to-one margin of source opinions. A female Episcopal priest criticized the Pope for his actions toward women: "The joke went around that he had been told he should step on the ground and kiss the women, and instead he kissed the ground and stepped on the women." (*Time* 2/4/85)

As was the case in the 1970s, debate over the ordination of women made up the bulk of discussion. In the 1980s, however, opinion was much more balanced, with 52 percent favoring ordination and 48 percent opposed. The Church still maintained its explanation of almost a decade earlier, this time in a statement from Pope John Paul. "[The Church] feels constrained by her faithfulness to the word of God as she understands it in the example of the Lord, the witness of Holy Scripture and a tradition of nearly 2,000 years, to exclude the ordination of women to the ministry of the priesthood." (*The Washington Post* 5/14/85) Archbishop John Foley echoed the same sentiment: "The ordination of women is not a concept emerging from sociological considerations. Jesus clearly did not ordain women to the priesthood, nor did He authorize the Church to do so." (*Time* 2/4/85)

Racial issues came into sharp focus during the 1980s, with ten opinions expressed about the Church's successes and failures. Debate on these issues came from both inside and outside the Church, with the faithful often pleading for improvements in the Church. For instance, an Hispanic parishioner said, "We need Hispanic priests who not only can speak our language, but understand our culture." (*The Washington Post* 7/6/86) A Fordham professor was more blunt in calling on black Christians to ". . . draw on Christian courage for a meaningful confrontation with racist institutions — all racist institutions including the Church." (*The Washington Post* 5/23/87) Our sampling period ended too early to capture the emerging debate generated by Father George Stallings' allegations of racism in the Church.

The most dramatic rise in discussion during the 1980s came in the area of free expression. We encountered 27 opinions in this arena of debate, more than during the previous two time periods combined. This was largely due to discussions of academic freedom and dissent connected to such high profile figures as Father Curran and Archbishop Hunthausen, along with Cardinal Ratzinger's push for greater theological conformity. In this area Church decisions and actions were rejected or criticized in 63 percent of all opinions. Catholic University was the source of some conflict when Archbishop Hickey vetoed the faculty choice for dean of the School of Religious Studies because of a dispute over sterilization. The faculty fired back angry, albeit anonymous, denunciations, in *The Washington Post*, "It's terrible, just terrible, because the guy is really a moderate. That's the vicious thing. It's such an insult to the whole theological faculty." (3/8/85) In 1984 a group of dissident nuns made news by signing an advertisement in *The New York Times* advocating a change in the Church stand on abortion. When the Vatican demanded that they publicly recant, the nuns responded with a widely publicized refusal: ". . . We believe that this Vatican action is a cause for scandal to Catholics everywhere. It seeks to stifle freedom of speech and public discussion in the Roman Catholic Church and create the appearance of consensus where none exists." (*Time* 1/7/85) Meanwhile some lay Catholics defended the Church's actions, ". . . there is a fine line between representing an institution and being your own free person." (*The Washington Post* 9/2/86)

The various outlets also presented somewhat different views of the status quo (see table 24, p. 132). CBS aired only ten opinions on these issues, six of which favored maintaining the status quo. That made CBS the only outlet where a majority of sources supported the status quo. Eight out of the ten statements dealt with the ordination of women, which was opposed by six of the eight sources.

At *Time*, 63 percent of opinions published favored a change in Church power structures. The magazine printed 32 statements of opinion, almost half of which dealt with the ordination of women. Women's ordination was discussed 15 times, followed by issues of the power of the laity, which were debated nine times. Discussions of dissent and freedom of expression were discussed by six sources. In the pages of *Time*, women's ordination was supported by a three-to-two margin. When it came to the laity, two out of every three sources quoted in *Time* favored giving the laity a larger, more powerful role. On issues of freedom of expression and dissent, sources in *Time* supported change by a two-to-one margin.

The New York Times carried a similar distribution of opinions, by a two-to-one margin (65 to 35 percent).

Majorities supported change on all issues that were debated. The *Times* carried 37 opinions on these issues. The largest area of discussion dealt with minority and women's issues. On the ordination of women, the 18 sources with opinions favored ordination by a two-to-one margin. In covering issues concerning the laity, only changes in the Mass received any attention in the *Times* sample. The eight opinions on these changes split five to three in favor of the updated liturgy. Issues of academic freedom and dissent were discussed five times, splitting three to two in favor of more freedom.

At *The Washington Post*, nearly two out of three sources (66 to 34 percent) favored changing the status quo. The *Post* gave greatest attention to minority and women's rights with 52 statements. On the specific issue of the ordination of women, 54 percent favored ordination. On racial issues all ten sources quoted criticized the Church. Among these statements, a picture emerged of a Church that is racist, has too little minority representation at any level, and needs to expand the role of minorities. In 1968 the *Post* reported that an organizer of the poor "urged the clergy and lay participants of the conference not to march into the ghettoes uninvited in what he called the 'traditional colonizing' manner of the Catholic Church." (8/22/68) The *Post* was also the only outlet to give significant attention to issues of freedom of expression. There were 37 opinions on academic freedom, dissent in the Church, and existence of the Index of Books. Two thirds of these opinions were critical of the Church's discipline and strictures.

Ecumenism

Relations between the Roman Catholic Church and other religions have undergone various strains for hundreds of years. In the spirit of Vatican II the Church made a committed effort to mend many of these fences and build greater religious unity. More frequent and convivial fellowship with other Christian communities was foremost on the agenda, but improving relations with Jews and Muslims also received attention.

To construct this dimension of news coverage, we coded opinions on: the desirability of Christian unity, obstacles to these unification efforts, the desirability of Catholic-Jewish relations, obstacles to improving Catholic-Jewish relations, appraisals of the state of Catholic relations with other religions, and any changes in those relationships. This group of opinions covers all aspects of the Catholic Church's outreach to non-Catholics. Later we will examine more specifically how the Second Vatican Ecumenical Council was presented in the press.

These discussions of interreligious relations were a significant point of debate, although at a much lower level than the first two themes. These issues together drew 105 statements, slightly more than half the level of discussion found on the power structure of the Church. This was also the only dimension on which there was a high degree of support for the Church. Overall, seven out of ten sources supported Church efforts to build unity and improve relations with other world religions. Moreover, support was strong across all groups of sources both within and outside the Church (see table 25, p. 133).

Even so, the broad support conceals a more balanced debate about the role of the Church in promoting Christian unity, as table 26 (p. 133) shows. When ecumenical outreach to other Christian faiths was discussed, it was unanimously supported (often by members of the hierarchy). When debate arose over the Church's teaching on this universally approved goal, however, half the sources criticized the Church as an obstacle to greater unity.

This margin of support was very stable over time (see table 27, p. 133). In the 1960s the 40 opinions reported split by more than two-to-one (68 percent) in favor of ecumenism. The 1970s saw this margin increase slightly as the number of opinions dropped. There were 28 opinions published or broadcast, and three-quarters of these supported efforts to improve interreligious ties. Discussion rose again in the 1980s, when 36 statements were made on the subject of interreligious relations. Nearly seven out of ten sources (69 percent) supported efforts to mend ecclesiastical fences.

In the 1960s, the most frequent point of debate was whether or not the Church was seen as an obstacle to Christian unity. This issue came up in 18 stories during the 1960s. Three out of five opinions saw the Church as an impediment. In the days of Vatican II, many Protestant leaders saw Catholic adherence to various theological traditions and some literal interpretations of the Bible as a significant hindrance to greater Christian fellowship. Disagreements over a variety of theological issues were cited four times, while the specific issue of Catholic indulgences was seen as a sticking point three times. Church opposition to birth control was mentioned twice as an obstacle to unity. Opposition to the office and primacy of the Pope was cited only once as a stumbling block to the formation of a unified church.

In general, these impediments were not seen as insoluble. When the subject of indulgences came up in the debates of Vatican II, Cardinal Sidarous of the Coptic Rite said, "the document should not have been brought up because indulgences were an obstacle to Christian unity." (*The Washington Post* 11/11/65) On other theological matters, Pope Paul VI put a positive light on a controversy with non-Catholics over the Roman Catholic Church's teachings on the Virgin Mary: ". . . it is consoling to see how many Christian brothers, still divided from us, look with greater serenity and objectivity at the Catholic doctrine on the Madonna; it is no longer for them 'the Catholic heresy.' Even if for them the Marian dogma still constitutes one of the major obstacles to union in the only faith with the Catholic Church." (*The New York Times* 5/11/67) A year later, however, a *Washington Post* reporter observed, "It appeared that recent efforts of Pope Paul VI for closer harmony between Roman Catholics and other Christian denominations could be set back by his conservative stand on birth control." (7/31/68)

For their part, defenders of the Church usually saw Catholic willingness to engage in dialogue and make some changes as eliminating obstacles. For instance, *The New York Times* reporter Robert Doty assessed the impact of a Vatican declaration on religious liberty: "Assuredly, it eliminates one more obstacle to dialogue and to the still remote but potential union between Catholic and non-Catholic Christians." (11/20/65) A few days later another *Times* reporter, John Cogley, noted the power of papal example in ecumenism: "The occasion marked the first time that a Pope had publicly participated in a service neither Protestant, Orthodox nor Roman Catholic but simply Christian. . . . The Pope's example, in the view of a number of theologians on the American bishops' press panel, will stimulate more inter-faith religious services throughout the world." (12/5/65)

While the debate over the role of the Church vis-a-vis Christian unity was generally unfavorable toward the Church, calls for unity were met with unanimous support among the ten sources that addressed the issue. At the very beginning of our study period, *The New York Times* quoted Pope Paul at length on his desire for unity among Christians: "The Pontiff said, 'the Catholic desire for

reunion with Protestantism is more alive than ever.'
Recommending ecumenical work with Protestants, he said
Catholics should 'not reproachfully recall past errors but
search for virtue, not wait for what has not happened in
four centuries but go out in a brotherly way and seek it'
[unity]." (3/9/64) In 1965 Pope Paul VI and Patriarch
Athenagoras mutually rescinded excommunication orders
that split their congregations. In closing their joint
statement, ". . . they joined in expressing the hope that
their gesture would be seen as an invitation to the entire
Christian world to seek the ultimate unity commanded by
Jesus when he said, 'That they may be one'." (*The New York
Times* 12/8/65) A simpler expression of support was given
by a Catholic teenager when asked how she felt about the
new emphasis on ecumenism, "How could you be a Catholic
and not believe in it?" (*The New York Times* 8/17/65).

On the other hand, the desirability of Catholic-Jewish
relations was mentioned only once in the 1960s sample.
When the Vatican II Council was drafting its declaration on
deicide, one monsignor said, "I hope and pray, once the
doctrine is promulgated, it will be the beginning of a new
era in relationships between Catholics and Jews." (*The
Washington Post* 12/7/64)

Assessing relations between Catholicism and other
religions occupied the attention of 11 sources during the
1960s. Five of these rendered opinions on the current shape
of interreligious ties, and the other six looked back to assess
how the relationship had changed. Appraisals of
interreligious ties were mixed. Three sources found the
current relationships solid or very good, while two viewed
interreligious relations as poor or marginal. An article in
Time noted the conviviality between Billy Graham and
Cardinal Cushing: "When evangelist Billy Graham
marched on Boston with his 'Crusade for Christ' last

month, Richard Cardinal Cushing, then in Rome, issued a statement welcoming him. Last week in Boston, Billy called on the Cardinal to thank him and the meeting turned into a regular love feast. . . . Said Billy: 'I feel closer to many Catholic traditions than I do to some of the most liberal Protestants.' Agreed the Cardinal: 'No Catholic can listen to you and not become a better Catholic.' " (10/16/64)

The conversion of Lucy Baines Johnson from the Episcopal Church to Catholicism met with much greater hostility. She requested and was granted a conditional baptism into Catholicism, implying in the eyes of some a lack of credibility in the Anglican rite. This led an Anglican Bishop to sermonize, ". . . Father Montgomery's decision to accede to Miss Johnson's request was a 'direct slap' at the Episcopal Church and 'a deliberate act denigrating another branch of Christendom.' Moreover, it was 'sacrilegious,' since to carry out an empty rite having no sacramental effect is an abuse of the sacrament. Bishop Pike called for an apology from the authorities of the Roman Catholic archdiocese of Washington." (*The New York Times* 7/11/65)

In the 1970s discussion of interreligious relations dropped off slightly, but opinions remained strongly in support of ecumenism. The leading point of debate was the desirability of Christian unity. Nine sources discussed these broad sentiments of fraternity and every one supported the idea. For instance, the U.S. Catholic-Anglican Consultation said that members "are convinced that this difference [over ordaining women] would not lead to a breakdown in efforts toward reunion of the churches, although it would introduce a new element." (*The New York Times* 11/7/75) An archbishop called for "corporate reunion," arguing, "Full agreement in doctrine is not needed before some measure of intercommunion is allowed' and concluded by calling for greater developments of joint Protestant-Catholic services." (*Time* 10/28/74)

The desirability of closer Catholic-Jewish relations was discussed by four sources, three of whom saw such ecumenism as desirable. For example, the Orthodox Jewish Congregations' resolution on interfaith dialogue acknowledged that "closer contact with other faith communities is salutary in facing the common grave challenges which threaten mankind's survival. . . ." (*The Washington Post* 12/3/76) Archbishop Baum commented, ". . . the interfaith conversation must focus not only on righting past wrongs and correcting past misunderstandings between Christians and Jews. We hope the dialogue . . . should result in a common mission — a positive contribution to the human spiritual need for meaning in a troubled world." (*The Washington Post* 11/13/75)

The view that the Church was an obstacle to Christian unity dropped in significance. It was debated by only eight sources during the 1970s, five of whom (62 percent) saw the Church as an obstacle to ecumenical efforts. The most commonly cited obstacles were the primacy of the papacy and Catholic refusal to ordain women to the priesthood, both mentioned three times. Among those who saw Church positions as a stumbling block was a member of the Vatican's Secretariat for Christian Unity. This unidentified cleric, when assessing the opposition of the Church to the ordination of women, remarked, "It's a pity that the Congregation [for the Doctrine of the Faith] did not see fit to consult us. In the future discussions with Anglicans, a lot will depend upon the nature of the arguments used. It will certainly hinder mutual recognition of ministers." (*Time* 2/7/77)

On the opposing side, *Time* magazine carried this unusual rebuttal of claims that papal primacy was an impediment to unity: ". . . a commission of 13 Catholic and 13 Lutheran theologians issued a remarkable statement. The issue of papal primacy, they said, 'need not be a barrier to reconciliation' of the Lutheran and Roman Catholic churches. . . . the latest paper states that 'Christ wills for his church a unity [that] must be manifest in the world' and concurs that a 'special responsibility for this may be entrusted to one individual minister, under the gospel.'. . . the Bishop of Rome might in the future function in ways useful to the broader Christian Church." (3/18/74)

Seven sources assessed the relationship between Catholicism and other world religions, and all but one saw those relations as good or improving. Relations with Jews were discussed five times, and relations with the Anglican Church supplied the two remaining comments. Not only were Catholic-Jewish relations the most discussed, the outlook was resoundingly positive, by a four-to-one margin. Pope Paul VI noted "the improvement that has taken place in Jewish-Catholic relations and expressed the hope that collaboration will continue to foster mutual understanding." (*The Washington Post* 12/3/76)

The 1980s saw a different picture emerge, as concerns shifted away from hopes for the future to measurements of the here and now. It was a time of reckoning for ecumenism, as 21 sources measured the current state of affairs or tracked what progress had been made. All but one of these assayers thought interreligious ties were good or improving. Most sources (17) marked the improvement in interreligious relations. Once again ties to Jews were discussed most frequently, appearing in 15 comments. All but one of these saw the situation as improving. For instance, Bishop John Keating remarked that Vatican II ". . . gave impetus to dialogue between Christians and Jews. Admittedly it has not eliminated all the tensions. But given the grimness of the history of the past 2,000 years and the tragic grimness of anti-Semitism, we are progressing swiftly." (*The Washington Post* 2/18/84)

The decision by Pope John Paul II to meet with Austrian President Kurt Waldheim occasioned controversy because of the latter's activities during World War II. Jewish leaders requested and were granted a meeting with the Pope to discuss the decision. A later meeting, in Miami during the Pope's U.S. visit, succeeded in convincing some Jewish leaders of the Pope's goodwill toward them. As one leader commented, "This is a very important meeting. It raises the Catholic-Jewish relationship to a new plateau and makes possible a better relationship in the future." (*The Washington Post* 9/2/87)

Catholic relations with Anglicans and Lutherans made up the balance of comments. *The Washington Post* quoted Pope John Paul II on reunion with the Lutheran communion: "Progress has been made to unite the churches again but 'we still experience anguish because full unity has not yet been achieved.' " In the same article, Bishop James Malone seconded these opinions: "It is almost like a love affair. Two people care for each other, are committed to each other. . ." (9/28/85)

Calls for Christian unity lagged far behind and were discussed by only four sources. Once again approval for these ecumenical ties was unanimous. Pope John Paul II was a frequent source of these comments, as evidenced in his hope for unity with Protestants, "It is my prayer to make the dawn of the third millennium the beginning of a special time for seeking full unity in Christ." (*The Washington Post* 9/28/85) Two years later he sounded an equally hopeful note on relations with the Eastern Orthodox Church: "Such a wealth of praise [for the Virgin Mary] could help us to hasten the day when the Church can begin once more to breathe fully with her 'two lungs' the East and the West." (*The Washington Post* 3/26/87)

In this new era, impediments to unity that were perceived as created by the Church were discussed five times. In the 1980s, the Church's treatment of dissenters was cited three times as an impediment to greater Christian unity. The ordination of women was said to be a sticking point by two sources, and residual opposition to the primacy of the Pope yielded one comment. In the mid-1980s relations between Catholics and Anglicans were particularly rosy, as they announced a joint draft of a declaration to resolve many of their theological differences. The goal of the declaration was to allow intercommunion of faiths, but *Post* reporter Marjorie Hyer saw a new problem: "by that time unity moves may be stalled on another thorny issue: ordination of women priests and possibly women bishops in some branches of Anglicanism, including the United States and Canada. . . . Anglican Bishop Mark Santer, co-chairman of the joint commission, called that issue a 'fresh and grave obstacle to reconciliation' because the Vatican has vetoed ordination of women." (*The Washington Post* 3/6/86)

Obstacles to Catholic-Jewish fellowship were discussed six times. Alleged Catholic sins of omission with regard to the Holocaust accounted for two references. Another source felt that the Vatican's refusal to recognize Israel was a stumbling block to good relations. The Pope's meeting with Austrian President Kurt Waldheim was the focus of the remaining three complaints. For instance, the World Jewish Congress ". . . called the announced meeting 'a tragedy for the Vatican and a sad day for Catholic-Jewish relations. This is the Pope who met with Arafat. This is the Pope who refuses to recognize Israel. This is not the first unsavory character the Pope has received in audience."

(*The Washington Post* 6/18/87) When a second Waldheim visit was announced a few months later, the *Post* reported that Rabbi Marc Tannenbaum noted "that the previously announced visit has caused 'widespread and grave concern' and said the meeting 'could have the most serious implications for Vatican-Jewish relations'." (*The Washington Post* 1/9/88)

There were considerable differences among the outlets studied in their treatment of ecumenism (see table 28, p. 134). As usual, CBS aired the fewest opinions on this issue. Three of the five opinions presented approved of efforts at ecumenism. *Time* featured over three times the amount of discussion found on CBS, with 17 statements pro and con. Of these, 65 percent favored improving ties among the world religions. In the pages of *Time*, the most heavily debated issue was whether the Catholic Church was an obstacle to unity. By a margin of five-to-two statements, *Time's* sources saw the Church as an impediment. On the other hand, support for Christian unity was unanimous among the four sources who mentioned it. Like all of its counterparts, sources in *Time* had few problems with the current state of interreligious relations and saw an improvement in relations. Three sources argued that relations had improved, while no one claimed to see a deterioration.

At *The Washington Post*, support for ecumenism ran even stronger, with 67 percent of sources supporting unity efforts among the 55 statements the *Post* printed on this set of issues. The top subject of debate at the *Post* was the claim that the Church was a hindrance to Christian unity, which was mentioned 17 times. Some aspect of Church theology or structure was seen as an obstacle by 65 percent of sources on this issue. Following close behind, with 16 mentions, were assessments of change in interreligious relations. These were overwhelmingly positive, with 94 percent of sources seeing increasing fellowship between the world's religions. Three other sources viewed the current state of ecumenical ties as good or healthy. As with *Time* magazine, sources in the *Post* were unanimous in their support for Christian unity. Efforts to improve Catholic-Jewish relations were approved of by a four-to-one margin, although four sources did see significant obstacles to those efforts.

Almost eight out of ten sources (79 percent) quoted on *The New York Times* voiced support for ecumenical efforts. The *Times* ran opinions on either side of the issue. Assessing interreligious relations was the largest source of copy, with 13 sources making judgments. Nine of these saw improvements in the connections between faiths, and none saw a downturn. Opinion was split, however, on the current state of affairs, with two seeing relations as good and two others finding evidence of a chill. All eight sources who discussed Christian unity agreed that this was a desirable goal for the Church. When it came to the debate over how the Catholic Church fit into plans for Christian unity, three sources saw the Church as an obstacle and three others disallowed such claims.

Of all the Church efforts to foster ecumenism, none was more dramatic than the convocation of Vatican II. This massing of Church leaders from around the world was convened by Pope John XXIII. It was charged with the specific tasks of renewing the Church and finding ways in which the Church could deal better with the modern world and other world religions. This monumental undertaking was completed in 1965, when Pope Paul VI called the Council closed. The Council was the subject of many news stories over the years.

Despite this attention, its work and decisions were the subject of far fewer evaluations than might have been expected. In the entire sample, only 12 sources assessed the success or failure of this unusual body.

As expected, most of this discussion took place during the 1960s, but there was some discussion on the twentieth anniversary of the Council. In the 1960s, the success of the Council was debated six times. Opinions were evenly split between those who viewed the sessions as a success and those who thought they fell short of their goal. Praise for the Council came in a *Time* report: "When Pope Paul closed [the Second Vatican Council] last week, he heralded it as 'among the greatest events of the Church.'" The reporter added, "Whatever the future's judgment, there can be little doubt that the council indeed represents a major and momentous step forward by carrying Christendom's oldest, largest body into modern times and bringing it into closer contact with all men — non-Catholic or not, Christian or not, religious or not." (*Time* 12/17/65)

Some tentative criticism occurred even before the Council was officially closed: "Already there are Catholics who complain that the Council is a failure for having avoided the real issues facing the Church — Christian unity and a radical revision of the Church's institutions and forms." More criticism came later as the Reverend James Kavanaugh proclaimed, "Nothing has really changed. We will continue to preserve the system that has paralyzed us." (*Time* 7/7/67)

The twentieth anniversary of the completion of the work of Vatican II was celebrated in 1985, and this prompted a new analysis of its declarations. Four sources had clear opinions on the success or failure of the Council, and once again they were split evenly. The Synod of Bishops, convened by the Pope to reflect on the state of the Church, issued a statement praising the Second Vatican Council: "All of us, bishops of the Oriental rites and the

Latin rite, have shared unanimously in a spirit of thanksgiving the conviction that the Second Vatican Council is a gift of God to the Church and to the world. . . . We see in it a wellspring offered by the Holy Spirit to the Church for the present and for the future." (*The New York Times* 12/8/85) Among the voices criticizing the Council was that of Cardinal Ratzinger. According to *Time*, "Ratzinger was a progressive advisor at Vatican II. Disillusioned with its aftermath, he turned conservative, and now says, 'Not all valid councils have proven, when tested by the facts of history, to have been useful.' " (2/4/85)

We were also interested in how the proceedings of the Council were presented to the outside world. Was the Council portrayed as a conference of Church leaders to resolve and reform various Church canons to modernize the Church, or were other motivations attributed to it? The only characterizations we found were made in the 1960s. Two sources argued that the sessions were really a battle between liberals and conservatives in the Church, while two others argued that they were an effort to modernize the Church.

The author of an unsigned *Time* magazine piece observed that prior to Vatican II ". . . the Church was scarcely facing up to the growing secularization of life, the explosion of science, the bitter claims to social justice in old nations and new. Catholic theology, dominated by a textbook scholasticism, appeared to have stopped in the 13th century. . . . Today that sort of thinking seems almost as remote in the Church as the sale of indulgences — and this is perhaps the strongest single measure of the Council's achievements." (12/17/65) On the other side *The Washington Post* observed, "Ecumenical Council liberals won decisive votes on new Church doctrine today. . . . The traditionalists, against the wishes of Pope Paul, had stiffened resistance to . . . a new co-leadership of the Church by the bishops together with the Pope. . . . The group failed in its last-ditch stand to mount an obstructionist vote. . . . The liberal victory appeared clear cut."

Assessments of the future of these reforms were also mixed. Of the four sources who assessed the future of the changes and reforms enacted by the Second Vatican Council, two argue that the Vatican would drag its heels to prevent their implementation. For example, *Time* blamed the Church's conservatism for a decline in the number of nuns: "Still other ex-sisters insist that they left precisely because their orders were not moving fast enough on the road to postconciliar reform. 'There seemed to be such a great conservatism and such a lack of promise from updating my community,' says one former nun, 'that I felt there was no point in waiting for the next 50 years.' . . . Unless the orders accelerate the pace of change,' believes one nun, 'the prospect is for even greater losses. Women who want to live committed Christian lives and are in orders that won't change, will have to leave to be true to their ideal." (1/13/67) One reporter argued that the reforms would be implemented, while Pope Paul VI argued that these reforms would lead to further reforms. Pope Paul 'calls the council not so much an end as a beginning. Paul has long promised to reform the Vatican's entrenched and antiquated Curia, a move the council also demanded. . . ." *Time* 12/7/65)

Church-State Relations

Discussions of the Catholic Church's relations with various levels of government in the United States received the least coverage of any dimension in the study. A total of 45 sources assessed the relationship between the Church and the state. To construct this dimension we looked for opinions on the following areas: assessments of threats to the separation of church and state, the use of tax revenues to underwrite parochial schools, the Church stand on the Vietnam war, Church stands on war in general, and discussions of the appropriateness of Church entanglements with the political system.

Opinion on this dimension was about evenly split, with 51 percent supporting the Church in its relations with government and 49 percent expressing some criticism. Over the course of time, however, opinion clearly turned against the Church (see table 29, p. 134). In the 1960s, almost three out of five opinions (58 to 42 percent) supported the Church's relations with secular authorities. In the 1970s, this proportion slipped slightly to 55 percent. By the 1980s, however, those who supported the Church's connections with secular politics had dropped to a minority of only 40 percent. CBS and *Time* had only eight evaluations combined in this phase, too few to generalize about (see table 30, p. 134). *The Washington Post* printed 20 opinions, which split evenly between support and criticism of the Church. *The New York Times* also split almost evenly in its 17 statements on church-state issues.

Whereas issues of sexual morality and Church authority tended to pit higher-ranking members of the Church hierarchy against all other sources, this set of issues produce a sharp division between clergy and non-clergy (see table 31, p. 135). Virtually every member of the clergy who was quoted (95 percent) upheld the Church teaching on issues involving church-state relations. Among the laity and non-Catholic sources, by contrast, five out of six (84 percent) opposed Church activities in the realm of secular politics.

Support for the Church's relations with the political world was bolstered by the Church's strictures on war. Opposition from within the Church's hierarchy to the war in Vietnam and war in general received significant media attention, almost all of it supportive. In the 1960s, eight out of ten sources expressed agreement with the Church's perceived opposition to the Vietnam conflict or war in general. These statements made up more than half of all opinions about church-state relations. In 1965, the recently elected Pope Paul VI rose to address the United Nations. He denounced war in what would become an often repeated statement, "Never one against the other, never again, never more. If you wish to be brothers, lay down weapons. One cannot love with offensive weapons in hand." (*Time* 10/15/65)

These efforts were not enough for some Catholics. Father Philip Berrigan and eight other Catholics denounced the Church: "We confront the Catholic Church, other Christian bodies and the synagogues of America with their silence and cowardice in the face of our country's crimes." (*The Washington Post* 5/27/68) Overall, however, these Church teachings were well received in the press, as evidenced by a Haynes Johnson column written over a decade later at the time of Paul's death: "As American combat forces first began moving through the elephant grass into action in Vietnam, he [Paul] journeyed to the United States and denounced war and militarism. As the world noted the 20th anniversary of the bombing of Hiroshima, he called for the outlawing of the manufacture and storage of nuclear weapons. . . ." (*The Washington Post* 8/9/78)

In the 1980s, a pastoral letter from the U.S. Conference of Bishops extrapolated from Pope Paul's lesson: "We remain convinced that the policy of nuclear deterrence is not a stable long term method of keeping the peace among sovereign states." All of this met with no criticism in the stories in our sample.

On domestic concerns, by contrast, few sources supported Church involvement in political affairs (see table

32, p. 135). Indeed, if opinions that discussed the Church teaching on either the Vietnam war or war in general are removed from the calculation, support for the Church drops sharply. Only two out of every five sources expressed support for the Church on this narrower dimension, compared to five out of six who praised its condemnation of war. What remains in the discussion are domestic issues like public funding for private schools, Church involvement in the politics of abortion legislation and other perceived threats to the separation of church and state. These issues were substantively different from concerns over war, so for the remainder of this section we will address only this narrower dimension.

With discussions of war removed from the analysis, criticisms of Church entanglements in politics held greater sway. Church involvement in politics was always seen as inappropriate, a threat to the separation of church and state. The number of opinions expressed about the proper relationship between sacred and secular authority increased sharply over the years. From only two opinions in the 1960s it tripled to six in the 1970s and doubled again in the 1980s to 12 statements. The margin of criticism also increased from the 1970s to the 1980s. In the 1970s critics outnumbered supporters by a two-to-one margin, and in the 1980s the margin widened to three-to-one.

During the 1970s Church involvement in debates over public funding for private schools and legalizing abortion drew attention. For example, on the issue of Church campaigns against legalized abortion, one layman remarked to *The New York Times*, "I make a distinction between religious and moral beliefs. The church should not try to force its religious beliefs on others, but I believe this is a moral issue, just like Vietnam. The issue then, as now, was: Is this the right way to treat our fellow man?" (*The New York Times* 3/19/78)

On the other side, the National Abortion Rights Action League objected to federal matching funds for an anti-abortion candidate since her candidacy "raises serious constitutional questions 'in light of the apparent direct institutional (involvement) of the Catholic Church in her campaign'." (*The Washington Post* 2/18/90)

The main reason for this increase in criticism in the 1980s was the Reagan administration's decision to extend diplomatic relations to the Holy See. Criticism abounded against a decision in which the Church had a relatively small role. Denunciations of this decision were numerous and sharp. In *The New York Times*, Reverend Jerry Falwell commented, "A bad precedent is being set. I wonder when Mecca will want one. I told the White House if they give one to the Pope, I may ask for one." Dr. James Dunn of the Baptist Joint Committee also attacked the decision: "We see it as a dangerous precedent for the United States of America to appoint an ambassador to a church. . . . it's a dumb, bungling move by an Administration that doesn't seem to understand the first lesson of church-state relations." (*The New York Times* 1/11/84) Criticism also came from the secular world, as reflected by Senator Ernest Hollings: "It's a violation of the First Amendment and sets a bad precedent." (*Time* 1/23/84)

Support for the decision was less resounding and sometimes defensive. For example, the *Times* quoted a spokesman for the Conference of Bishops: ". . . the decision to send an ambassador to the Vatican was not a church-state issue and 'confers no special privilege or status on the Church.'" (*The New York Times* 1/11/84)

Church efforts to encourage the outlawing of abortion remained a point of contention, particularly when several Church leaders called on Catholic politicians to vote according to Church teaching. This brought angry responses from prominent Catholic politicians, most notably Mario Cuomo and Geraldine Ferraro. During the 1984 campaign, Dan Rather quoted Geraldine Ferraro: ". . . when I speak out I am doing my duty as a public official. And my foremost duty is to uphold the Constitution, which guarantees freedom of religion." (CBS 9/10/84) Cardinal Bernardin defended the Church's stance, "In this matter there is no dichotomy in reality — and there should be none in the practice of individuals or society — between the private stance of persons and their public responsibility, or between private and public morality." (*The New York Times* 9/28/84)

Summary

To summarize briefly a wide range of findings, opinions in the media were tilted against the Church's teaching on issues involving sexual morality and authority relations within the Church, and its involvement in secular politics (aside from support for Church statements opposing war). Only on the relatively non-controversial issue of ecumenical outreach did the Church receive support from a majority of sources. The distribution of opinion varied according to the media outlet, time period, and the position of the source of opinion vis-a-vis the Church. A more detailed summary appears at the conclusion of this report.

Characterizing the Church

THE CHURCH IS more than the sum of its teachings, just as the news is more than the sum of the opinions that appear. Thus, the media's depiction of the Catholic Church involves not only its presentation of policy issues in which the Church is involved. It also reflects the tone of news accounts, which is strongly influenced by the use of descriptive language. For example, the tone of a story might be discursive, sarcastic, or ironic, depending upon the language chosen to convey the same factual information.

We looked earlier at another contributor to the tone of news accounts, the presence or absence of conflictual material (i.e., is the Church's teaching presented without debate, or do critics also have their say?). But the use of language is probably the most significant factor in the tone of news coverage, as the actual medium that shapes the communicative enterprise. The entire journalistic endeavor is an attempt to describe events and ideas that the audience cannot experience directly. It is language (and, in the case of television, pictures) that guides the audience's vicarious experience of the reality that journalism describes.

Our study concentrated on the use of descriptive terms that labeled or characterized the Church and its representatives. In contrast to determining the balance of opinions on particular issues, this represents a means of measuring more general depictions of Catholicism. We were especially interested in words or phrases that carry emotive, judgmental, or value-laden connotations. To create the list of likely terms, we noted any use of emotive, colorful, or judgmental language while performing our initial qualitative analysis of the news. This list was then augmented by use of a thesaurus to identify synonyms and antonyms. The resulting list consisted largely of terms that fell along three descriptive dimensions: ideology (liberal vs. conservative), control (oppressive vs. liberating), and relevance (relevant vs. irrelevant).

In order to ensure that these words could be meaningfully assigned to a particular dimension, ten people were asked to sort the words into six groups, representing the opposite poles of the three dimensions. Their only instructions were to place each word in the group they felt it most closely resembled. Those words which were not placed in the same position by at least seven out of the ten judges were excluded from the analysis as overly ambiguous.

This procedure produced three separate lists of words and phrases that were arranged as pairs of opposites dealing with the Church's ideology, authority, and relevance. These dimensions provided a means of measuring media descriptions of ideology in the Church, authority and control in the Church, and the Church's relevance to the modern world. Coders counted the number of words used along each dimension and their placement on one side or the other. By counting these words or phrases, we were able to assess the balance of descriptive language along the major dimensions on which the Church was characterized.

The first dimension — ideology — noted conservative and liberal terms. On the conservative end were words like "reactionary," "retrogressive," and "traditional," while on the liberal side were "radical," "progressive," and "revolutionary." This dimension came into play most frequently when stories attempted to characterize papal candidates or new appointees for any job. For example, *The New York Times* summed up internecine battles in the Church, "Moderate and conservative bishops suggest that because the liberals have confronted the Vatican so publicly, the liberal voice has seemed dominant and more moderate and conservative prelates' voice has often been drowned out." (12/1/86)

The second dimension separated words according to their characterization of the type of control exercised by the Church. On the "oppressive" end of this spectrum were such terms as "authoritarian," "fascist," "rigid," and "iron-handed"; on the opposite side were terms like "liberating," "unrestrictive," and "emancipating." For example, a *New York Times* reporter observed, "The bishops have repudiated Rome's authoritarian heritage on the conscious level. But their loathing for abortion has overwhelmed their judgment and their authoritarian instincts have seized control." (1/16/77)

The final dimension identified words that connoted something about the relevance of the Church in the world. Words connoting irrelevance were terms such as "useless," "outdated," "anachronistic," and "medieval." On the opposite end of the spectrum were terms like "useful," "relevant," and "in touch." For instance, one source criticized the encyclical *Humanae Vitae* for ". . . throwing us back into the Middle Ages. . . ." (*Time* 5/24/76)

Rather than count every emotive term that appeared, we measured the balance of such terms in each story. That is, we asked whether an entire story tended to characterize the Church mainly as liberal or conservative, liberating or oppressive, relevant or out of touch. Following previous scholarship, we adhered to a "two to one rule" in making this judgment. If twice as many words were drawn from one end of a dimension as from the other, the story was coded as tilted in that direction. The story was also coded if terms from only one end of a given dimension were used.

About one out of four stories (456 in all) characterized the Church on one of the three dimensions. The most common labels were ideological, describing the Church along a liberal to conservative continuum. A total of 396 stories included one or more of these terms. Less frequent (appearing in 123 stories) were characterizations of the forms of control in the Church. Least common were descriptions of the Church's relevance, which appeared in 64 stories.

There were sizable differences in the rate of

characterization among outlets. *Time* magazine led the pack, with half of its stories using one or more emotive or judgmental terms. This reflects the stylistic approach common to newsmagazines, which employ more judgmental and sometimes more flamboyant language than daily journalism typically permits. Second was *The Washington Post*, where 22 percent of stories used such terms. Close behind was *The New York Times*, where 20 percent of stories were coded along at least one of the three dimensions. CBS was the least likely to characterize the Church along these dimensions, with only 15 percent of stories relying on such language.

Ideology

Among those stories that clearly favored terms indicating a conservative or liberal label for the Church, almost two thirds (63 percent) described the Church or its leaders as conservative, compared to only 37 percent that described the Church as liberal. There were substantial differences in ideological labeling, both among outlets and over time. Nonetheless, a majority of stories employing ideological language stressed the Church's conservatism in all outlets and time periods studied.

Stories on CBS were the most likely to present the Church as conservative, by a margin of three to one (see table 33). After the death of Pope Paul, a CBS reporter reflected on the use of ideological terms to describe papal candidates, ". . . words like liberal and conservative, progressive and traditional. These are rough labels. Usually ill-fitting and nearly always misleading. Pope John was an old fashioned man in many ways, who threw open the doors of the Church to the fresh air of new times." The story that followed that same night showed no such self-consciousness when it quoted a British Catholic writer as saying, "Paul had put the Church on the brink of disaster by alienating both liberals and conservatives." (8/7/78)

Time was close behind, with stories favoring conservative terms outpacing those using mainly liberal words by almost a three-to-one ratio (74 vs. 26 percent). This ratio is the result of *Time's* style of layering descriptive terms in a story. A 1968 article provides an illustration, "Despite Paul's admirably progressive reform of the Curia, the men who administer it are still for the most part conservative. . . . His chief assistant is the equally reactionary Archbishop Giovanni Benelli. . . . At the same time, some liberal prelates named by Paul to the Curia have found themselves stymied by conservative peers." (11/22/68) *The New York Times* was right on the average for all outlets, describing the Church mainly as conservative in 63 percent of stories and liberal 37 percent of the time. *The Washington Post* came closest to a balanced use of ideological language, with 53 percent of its stories connoting conservatism in the Church and 47 percent identifying the Church with liberal labels.

The tendency to emphasize the Church's conservatism increased during the 1970s (see table 34, p. 136). During the 1960s, stories favoring conservative characterizations had outpaced liberal ones by just under a three-to-two margin (59 to 41 percent). In the 1970s, that gap widened to two-to-one (66 to 34 percent). This change in language was greatly affected by efforts to describe likely candidates for Pope after the death of Pope Paul VI. The papabili were frequently described in terms of their conservatism, often to note how few progressives or liberals were in the running. *Time* described the field of candidates in the following passage: "The candidates form a mass of middle-roaders with muted political coloration. There are no out-and-out progressives, but neither are there any papal possibilities

in the mold of the fervently right wing Ottaviani. . ."
(8/21/78). This balance held steady during the 1980s, when
65 percent of all labels described the Church as
conservative.

Authority

The Church was overwhelmingly portrayed as an
oppressive or authoritarian institution. Among stories
whose language clearly favored one side or the other of this
dimension, 85 percent described the Church as oppressive.
This discussion was most affected by reports on the
Church's handling of dissent. Once again, this portrayal
predominated among all outlets and time periods, though to
varying degrees.

Most likely to present the Church as oppressive was
The Washington Post, where over nine out of ten stories (90
percent) that employed such characterizations emphasized
its authoritarian nature (see table 35, p. 136). For instance,
in analyzing the first few months of Pope John Paul II's
reign a *Post* reporter observed, "in the approximately 60
addresses and speeches he has given . . . the Pope already
has stamped firmly on the Church his belief in rigid
orthodoxy." (12/9/78) The *Post* also carried the largest
number of stories (51) that made such characterizations.
This coincides with the *Post's* attention to power relations
within the Church.

Time followed with 40 stories, of which 82 percent made
characterizations connoting oppressiveness in the Church.
At *The New York Times*, there were 26 such stories; those
with oppressive connotations outdistanced those with
liberating ones by a three-to-one margin. CBS used such
characterizations only six times. In every case, however,
the story emphasized the Church's oppressiveness.

Over the course of time the Church was increasingly

portrayed in this light (see table 36, p. 136). In the 1960s, stories presenting the Church as oppressive dominated by a three-to-one margin. Church efforts to rein in dissent on such issues as celibacy and birth control drew many of these characterizations. In the 1970s, the gap widened to almost four to one, as the Church dealt with new dissent over the rights of women and minorities. By the 1980s a remarkable unanimity of description prevailed in media accounts. Forty stories used the language of oppression to describe the Church, while no story ever described it as liberating. Disciplinary actions against dissidents like Father Curran contributed heavily to these characterizations. For instance, *Time* quoted Father Curran's reaction to such acts: "Authoritarianism makes everything of the same importance, whether it's central to the faith or not. . . ."

Relevance

Characterizations of the Church's relevance appeared least often. When they were used, however, a familiar imbalance prevailed. An institution that was usually described as conservative and oppressive was also presented most often as irrelevant. Once again the margin exceeded two to one, this time by 68 to 32 percent of stories employing such language. And once again, this imbalance held for all times and places included in the study. Among the four outlets, *Time* emphasized the Church's irrelevance most frequently, employing this term or a synonym in 83 percent of its stories (see table 37, p. 136). Again, the frequent use of emotive terms set the tone for *Time* stories. When debates arose over Church handling of dissent, *Time* asserted, "The debates in St. Peter's have made it clear that it is no sin to question outdated traditions. . . There are plenty of theologians who feel that such blunt methods are as obsolete as the Inquisition, and derive from an outdated understanding of the Church. . ." (3/19/65) Two years later, *Time* observed, "An increasing number of U.S. Catholics consider compulsory Mass on Sunday an unnecessary chore as anachronistic as meatless Fridays." (4/21/67) Nearly three out of five newspaper stories that characterized the Church on this dimension presented it as irrelevant — 59 percent at the *Post* and 58 percent at the *Times*. Once again, CBS contained the fewest references, but four out of five stories (80 percent) stressed the Church's lack of relevance.

The Church's lack of relevance was emphasized most heavily in recent years (see table 38, p. 137). It was described as an outdated institution in four out of five stories during the 1980s, compared to three out of five during the 1970s and two out of three during the 1960s. For example, a *New York Times* reporter commented on Pope John Paul's renewed emphasis on traditional devotions, "The reaction of more modern or progressive Catholics to all of this is mixed, with some finding the devotions a bit antique and embarrassing." (7/18/86)

In sum, the linguistic tone of news coverage has been generally (and increasingly) unfavorable to the Church. At every outlet, and during every time period, it was usually portrayed as an oppressive or authoritarian institution with little relevance for the contemporary world. In addition, the Church was frequently (and increasingly) labeled as a conservative institution. This ideological labeling lacks the negative valence of the other dimensions (except where judgmental terms like "progressive" and "reactionary" were used), but it accords with the media's tendency to portray the Church as rigid and out of touch with modern times.

Conclusion

A 1965 *TIME* article on the changing mood within the Catholic Church also provided a portent for the changing tenor of media coverage. *Time* commented: ". . . nothing nowadays is sacred in the new climate of freedom within the Church: unspoken thoughts of yesteryear are headline snarls today." (9/24/65)

The headlines may not always have snarled since then, but the coverage has rarely lost its bite. Our study of news coverage during the post-Vatican II era found the Church on the losing side of the battle of ideas, an institution depicted as conservative, oppressive, and out of touch with the modern world. This media portrayal was not the result of advocacy or adversarial journalism of the type that might be found in opinion journals (like the *New Republic* or *National Review*), sensationalistic tabloids, or nativist pamphlets. Instead it reflected the balance of opinions and linguistic devices that comprised the generally straightforward and factual accounts of America's leading national media outlets over the past quarter century.

The news was certainly not all bad for the Church. The study found that members of the hierarchy were heavily cited; official teachings were frequently presented, most often without refutation by critics; and on some issues, ranging from abortion and homosexuality to ecumenism and questions of war and peace, the Church's teaching was endorsed by a majority of sources whose opinions were printed or broadcast.

Overall, however, the negatives for the Church outweighed the positives. On most controversies involving Catholic teachings, the Church came out on the losing side of the issue debate reported in the media. Although the opinion breakdown varied from one issue to another, sources supporting the Church were in the minority on the broad range of debates involving sexual morality and Church authority that dominated the coverage. These included heated controversies over birth control, clerical celibacy, the role of women and minorities in the Church, and the Church's response to internal dissent and issues involving freedom of expression.

The major exception to this pattern involved ecumenical efforts, which the media treated as a kind of "motherhood and apple pie" issue, supported by all people of good will. Even on this dimension, however, opinion was split over whether the Church was helping or hindering efforts to promote interreligious unity. Similarly, opinion was about evenly divided on the Church's involvement in political affairs. But most of the praise was for Church pronouncements condemning war. On domestic disputes over church-state relations, most sources opposed the Church's doctrines or activities.

How could the balance of opinions tilt against the Church despite the media's extensive reporting of Church teachings and reliance on the hierarchy as sources of information? The answer directs our attention to the structure of the coverage. Controversial issues were frequently presented as conflicts between the Church hierarchy, on one side, and lower-level clergy, lay Catholics, and non-Catholics, on the other. Journalists frequently approached this subject matter from a secular vantage point, structuring their coverage along the familiar lines of political reportage. Debates were structured less in terms of religious significance than as conflicts between authorities and dissidents, outsiders and insiders, those in charge and those who wanted new policies or more power.

The result was a long-running media drama that pitted a hide-bound institutional hierarchy against reformers from within and without. This portrayal was reinforced by the language used to describe the Church in media accounts. The descriptive terms most frequently applied to the Church emphasized its conservative ideology, authoritarian forms of control, and anachronistic approach to contemporary society.

In many respects, moreover, long-term trends in the coverage have been less than favorable to the Church. The sheer volume of coverage has dropped sharply since the 1960s, even as its topical focus has gradually diverged from the perspectives of Catholic editors (as reported in Catholic News Service surveys). Official Church teachings are reported less frequently and are challenged more often when they do appear. Finally, the language used to describe the Church increasingly carries connotations of conservatism, oppressiveness, and irrelevance. Ironically, the only major dimension of the coverage that has remained reasonably stable over time is the issue debate. The Church may not fare especially well in the battle of ideas, but it has not fared worse over time.

Indeed, the more conflictual and negativistic tone of recent news coverage may have less to do with the media's image of the Church than with changes in the journalistic profession and the larger society. American culture has undergone a populist upsurge since the mid-1960s, with insurgent movements on both sides of the political spectrum attacking institutional authority on many fronts. During the same period, journalistic standards have shifted away from the goal of neutral, factual, dispassionate reportage to a more interpretive, critical, and socially engaged approach. Since the political culture of major media journalism is strongly secular and egalitarian, these tendencies have probably colored the tone of news coverage.

To a great degree, of course, the changing mixture of topics, sources, and arguments presented in the news reflects changes in reality, i.e., the Church's situation, the issues and challenges confronting it, and the individuals who give this institution its human face. As this study has shown, however, a news story consists of much more than the facts it relates. The news is less like a mirror of reality than a prism that breaks up a single object into multiple images. Those images then become the reality that is experienced by the news audience.

Subjective elements enter the news from the moment a story is assigned (and another is ignored) until the resulting article or broadcast is edited and a headline or anchor lead-in is added to the finished product.

In addition to story selection, the areas in which interpretation take place include the choice of sources to rely upon, the use of language and pictures, the order in which information is presented, and the facts and opinions that are included or excluded. Further, journalism is a group enterprise in which different people may suggest a news topic, assign it as a story, research it, write (or film) it, and edit it for final presentation.

The most obvious evidence for the importance of subjective factors in shaping the news comes from differences in coverage at various media outlets. For example, an individual whose knowledge of the Church came from regular viewing of the CBS Evening News would come away with dramatically different impressions from those of a subscriber to *Time* magazine. Among the four media outlets in the study, CBS focused most heavily on the papacy and least heavily on social conflicts involving the Church. When opinions on social controversies were aired, they were consistently more favorable to the Church's teaching than in the other outlets. (For example, CBS was the only outlet to present a majority of supporting opinion on issues involving power relations in the Church.)

And the network was the outlet least likely to use judgmental language, which tended to depict the Church in a negative light.

By contrast, *Time* paid the most attention to dissidents and focused most heavily on conflict, featured the most frequent use of judgmental language (and led the pack in depicting the Church as irrelevant), and printed a majority of opinions opposed to the Church on every issue dimension except ecumenism. *Time's* readers received the image of a Church that was much more besieged, conflict-ridden, and on the wrong side of the issues than the Church observed by CBS viewers.

These sharp differences in tone stem at least partly from institutional differences in the depiction of news. Television's need for visual material leads to an emphasis on pomp and circumstance, which Church rituals and papal visits provide in abundance. Television's time constraints also limit the attention the medium can pay to internal disputes in the Church and its role in broader social controversies. And television tends to rely on established institutional sources who are readily accessible and familiar with the medium's special demands for succinct and vivid verbal images.

In contrast, *Time* covers the Church as part of a regular religion beat, and its weekly deadlines encourage a search for more diverse topical and source material. The traditions of magazine journalism also permit more colorful and judgmental presentations of social controversies than daily news features, at least in the national media. *Time's* stories are typically structured around conflicts that present heated debate and often side with one participant against the other. All this made for a more emotive, conflictual, and negative portrayal of the Church.

This is not to say that one portrayal was more correct or

closer to reality than the other. Both illustrate the importance of news judgment in constructing media images of reality. Ultimately, journalists are less fact collectors than storytellers. The stories they tell become, to a large extent, the reality that we experience. And the stories they tell about the Catholic Church rely on politics as much as religion for their dramatic appeal. Over the years, the plots have focused on bureaucratic infighting, political intrigues, styles of leadership, policy disputes, and the battle for public opinion. Increasingly, the storyline revolves around a beleaguered authority struggling to enforce its traditions and decrees on a reluctant constituency.

Endnotes

1. Michael Schwartz, *The Persistent Prejudice* (Huntington, Ind., 1984), p. 137.
2. *Ibid,* p. 136.
3. S. Robert Lichter, Stanley Rothman, and Linda S. Lichter, *The Media Elite* (Bethesda, Md., 1986), p. 22.
4. Our estimates of coverage were based on a preliminary examination of the *Times'* and *Post's* own news indices. The *Post* did not yet index its coverage during the 1960s, and its index is organized somewhat differently than that of the *Times*. In the event, our actual inspection of *Post* articles on microfiche revealed a higher rate of coverage of the Church than we had anticipated. As a result, the *Post* is somewhat overrepresented in our sample relative to the *Times*. To insure that this does not affect interpretation of the overall results, the text breaks down all major findings according to media outlet, pointing out differences among outlets as well as overall patterns of coverage.

Tables

Table 1
Total Number of Stories for each Outlet by Era

	1960s Number of Stories	1970s Number of Stories	1980s Number of Stories	Total Number of Stories
CBS	+	126	105	231
Time	146	70	43	259
Washington Post*	1705	1265	1200	4170
New York Times*	2840	1310	1370	5520
				10,180

+Note: Broadcasts no longer available for inspection.
*Note: Study analyzed random samples of articles.

Table 2
Top Ten Topics

		Number of Stories
1)	Church happenings	550
2)	News of the Pope	229
3)	Relations with other religions	176
4)	Dissent within the Church	164
5)	Education	150
6)	Canon Law	136
7)	Birth control	132
8)	Abortion	104
9)	Civil Rights	86
10)	Church in politics	83

Table 3

Top Ten Topics in each Era

1960s	Number of Stories	Percent of Stories
1) Church happenings	238	31
2) Birth control	106	14
3) Changes in Canon Law	95	12
4) Relations with other religions	82	11
5) Dissent within the Church	81	11
6) Education	68	9
7) Civil Rights	53	7
8) News of the Pope	46	6
9) Vietnam war	41	5
10) Economic issues	30	4

1970s	Number of Stories	Percent of Stories
1) Church happenings	161	28
2) News of the Pope	112	19
3) Abortion	57	10
4) Relations with other religions	46	8
5) Education	43	7
6) Church in politics	40	7
7) Women's issues	39	7
8) Changes in Canon Law	33	6
9) Crimes by clerics	21	4
10) Dissent within the Church	20	3

1980s	Number of Stories	Percent of Stories
1) Church happenings	152	29
2) News of the Pope	71	14
3) Dissent within the Church	63	12
4) Relations with other religions	48	9
5) Abortion	41	8
6) Education	39	7
7) Economic issues	37	7
8) Church in politics	36	7
9) Women's issues	27	5
10) Homosexuality	21	4

Table 4

Top Ten Topics in each Outlet

CBS	Number of Stories	Percent of Stories
1) News of the Pope	94	41
2) Church happenings	59	26
3) Abortion	22	9
4) Church in politics	16	7
5) Dissent in the Church	10	4
6) Relations between religions	8	4
7) War	6	3
7) Economic issues	6	3
9) Education	5	2
9) Changes in Canon Law	5	2
9) Divorce	5	2
9) Church and the media	5	2

Time	Number of Stories	Percent of Stories
1) Church happenings	79	30
2) Changes in Canon Law	44	17
3) Dissent in the Church	38	15
4) News of the Pope	32	12
5) Birth control	23	9
6) Relations between religions	22	8
7) Education	17	7
8) Abortion	13	5
9) Women's issues	11	4
10) Priestly celibacy	10	4

Washington Post	Number of Stories	Percent of Stories
1) Church happenings	253	30
2) Relations between religions	88	11
3) Dissent with in the Church	76	9
3) Education	76	9
5) News of the Pope	68	8
6) Birth control	65	8
7) Changes in Canon Law	49	6
8) Civil rights	47	6

Table 4 (Cont.)

Washington Post	Number of Stories	Percent of Stories
9) Economic issues	45	5
10) Women's issues	38	5

New York Times	Number of Stories	Percent of Stories
1) Church happenings	159	29
2) Relations between religions	58	11
3) Education	52	9
4) Birth control	41	8
5) Dissent within the Church	40	7
6) Abortion	39	7
7) Changes in Canon Law	38	7
8) News of the Pope	35	6
9) Civil rights	31	6
10) Church in politics	26	5

Table 5

Comparisons of Topical Coverage
1960s

Study Results	Catholic Editors' Picks
1) Church happenings	1) Changes in Canon Law
2) Birth control	2) News of the Pope
3) Changes in Canon Law	3) Ecumenism
4) Ecumenism	4) Birth Control
5) Dissent in the Church	5) Dissent in the Church
6) Education	6) Church happenings
7) Civil Rights	7) Civil Rights
8) News of the Pope	8) Vietnam War
9) Vietnam War	9) Peace efforts
10) Economic Issues	10) Celibacy

1970s

1) Church happenings	1) Church happenings
2) News of the Pope	2) Church in politics
3) Abortion	3) Abortion

Media Coverage of the Catholic Church

Table 5 (Cont.)
1960s

Study Results	Catholic Editors' Picks
4) Ecumenism	4) Changes in Canon Law
5) Education	5) Women's Issues
6) Church in Politics	6) Hunger relief
7) Women's issues	7) Divorce
8) Changes in Canon Law	8) Dissent in the Church
9) Crimes by clerics	9) Education
10) Dissent in the Church	10) Euthanasia

1980s

1) Church happenings	1) Church in politics
2) News of the Pope	2) News of the Pope
3) Dissent in the church	3) Abortion
4) Ecumenism	4) Economic Issues
5) Abortion	5) Dissent in the Church
6) Economic Issues	6) Maintaining religious
7) Education	7) Ecumenism
8) Church in politics	8) Hunger relief
9) Women's issues	9) Changes in Canon Law
10) Homosexuality	10) Family Farms

Table 6
Sources Cited in Stories about the Catholic Church

	Number of Citations
Church hierarchy	2201
Priests and religious	810
Lay Catholics	510
Catholic schools	305
Catholic media	109
Catholic dissidents	43
Total Catholic sources	3978
Leaders of other churches	297
Federal government	205
State/local governments	140

Table 6 (Cont.)

	Number of Citations
Foreign governments	46
Abortion rights groups	28
All others	950
Total Non-Catholic sources	1666

Table 7
Top Twenty Individuals Cited in Stories on the Catholic Church

		Number of Citations
1)	Pope Paul VI	228
2)	Pope John Paul II	107
3)	Cardinal Bernardin	51
4)	Cardinal O'Connor	39
5)	Cardinal O'Boyle	32
6)	Father Charles Curran	30
7)	Bishop Malone	28
8)	Cardinal Cooke	25
8)	Cardinal Cushing	25
10)	Father Andrew Greeley	21
11)	Cardinal Krol	19
11)	Cardinal Spellman	19
13)	Cardinal Shehan	16
14)	Cardinal Ratzinger	15
14)	Cardinal Hickey	15
16)	Cardinal Cody	14
16)	Archbishop Dearden	14
16)	Archbishop Weakland	14
19)	Pope John Paul I	13
19)	Hans Küng	13

Table 8

Use of Sources in Stories about the Catholic Church by Outlet

	CBS	Time	Wash Post	NY Times	All Outlets
	%	%	%	%	%
Church hierarchy	38	43	38	39	39
Priests and other religious	9	16	15	14	14
Lay Catholics	3	9	10	10	10
Catholic schools	8	6	6	5	5
Catholic media	1	2	2	2	2
Catholic dissidents+	*	2	1	1	*
Other churches	4	4	6	6	5
Federal government	10	2	3	3	4
State/local gov't.	2	1	2	4	2
Foreign government	*	1	1	*	*
All others	25	14	16	16	18
	100%	100%	100%	100%	100%
Number of Sources	542	1197	2300	1605	5644

*Note: Less than 0.5 percent

+Note: Reverend Charles Curran and Reverend Hans Küng

Table 9

Presentation of the Church Position by Era

	1960s Percent of Stories	1970s Percent of Stories	1980s Percent of Stories
Church position presented	43	40	37
Catholic clergy positions presented	31	32	44
No position	26	28	19
	100%	100%	100%
Number of Stories	771	580	525

Table 10
Presence of Debate in Stories Identifying the Church Position

	Church position presented Percent of Stories	Catholic clergy view presented Percent of Stories	No View Percent of Stories
No debate	50	65	91
Internal debate	39	23	4
Other critics	11	12	5
	100%	100%	100%
Number of Stories	763	648	465

Table 11
Debate of Church Positions by Outlet

	Debate Percent of Stories	No Debate Percent of Stories		Number of Stories
Time	69	31	100%	116
Washington Post	52	48	100%	351
New York Times	49	51	100%	195
CBS	25	75	100%	101
All Outlets	50	50	100%	763

Table 12
Debate of Church Positions by Era

	Debate Percent of Stories	No debate Percent of Stories		Number of Stories
1960s	49	51	100%	335
1970s	43	57	100%	233
1980s	58	42	100%	195

Table 13
Areas of Debate by Outlet

	CBS %	Time %	Wash Post %	NY Times %	All Outlets %
Sexual Morality	25	42	22	36	30
Power Structures	16	19	30	16	22

Table 13 (Cont.)
Areas of Debate by Outlet

	CBS	Time	Wash Post	NY Times	All Outlets
	%	%	%	%	%
Ecumenism	11	9	14	9	13
Church-State	8	2	6	7	5
All others	40	28	28	32	32
	100%	100%	100%	100%	100%
Number of Opinions	64	170	357	234	825

Table 14
Viewpoints on Sexual Morality by Outlet

	Support Percent of Views	Criticize Percent of Views		Number of Opinions
CBS	69	31	100%	16
Time	38	62	100%	71
Washington Post	32	68	100%	78
New York Times	56	44	100%	84
All Outlets	44	56	100%	249

Note: Based on sources expressing an explicit opinion on the Church's teaching.

Table 15
Viewpoints on Sexual Morality by Source Type

	Agree Percent of Views	Disagree Percent of Views		Number of Opinions
Church Hierarchy	88	12	100%	106
Priests and religious	9	91	100%	57
Laity	14	86	100%	59
All Others	15	85	100%	27
Overall	44	56	100%	249

Note: Based on sources expressing an explicit opinion on the Church's teaching.

Table 16

Viewpoints on Sexual Morality by Era

	Support Percent of Views	Criticize Percent of Views		Number of Opinions
1960s	36	64	100%	132
1970s	56	44	100%	52
1980s	52	48	100%	65

Note: Based on sources expressing explicit opinion on the Church's teaching.

Table 17

Viewpoints on Church Teachings on Sexual Morality

	Support Church Percent of Views	Oppose Church Percent of Views		Number of Opinions
Homosexuality	67	33	100%	15
Artificial Reproduction	67	33	100%	6
Abortion	56	44	100%	34
Birth Control	47	53	100%	124
Celibacy	27	73	100%	70

Note: Based on sources expressing an explicit opinion on the Church's teaching.

Table 18

Viewpoints on Birth Control by Source Type

	Agree Percent of Views	Disagree Percent of Views		Number of Opinions
Church Hierarchy	85	15	100%	60
Priests and religious	10	90	100%	20
Laity	7	93	100%	27
All Others	18	82	100%	17
Overall	47	53	100%	124

Note: Based on sources expressing an explicit opinion on the Church's teaching.

Table 19

Viewpoints on Abortion by Outlet

	Agree Percent of Views	Disagree Percent of Views		Number of Opinions
CBS	60	40	100%	5
Time	33	67	100%	9
Washington Post	40	60	100%	5
New York Times	74	26	100%	15
All Outlets	56	44	100%	34

Note: Based on sources expressing an explicit opinion on the Church's teaching.

Table 20

Viewpoints on the Church Power Structure by Era

	Favor Change Percent of Views	Favor Status Quo Percent of Views		Number of Opinions
1960s	66	34	100%	38
1970s	66	34	100%	71
1980s	60	40	100%	75

Note: Based on sources expressing an explicit opinion on the Church's position.

Table 21

Viewpoints on the Church Power Structure by Source Type

	Favor Change Percent of Views	Favor Status Quo Percent of Views		Number of Opinions
Church Hierarchy	35	65	100%	52
Priests and religious	78	22	100%	37
Laity	69	31	100%	75
All Others	91	9	100%	21
Overall	64	36	100%	185

Note: Based on sources expressing an explicit opinion on the Church's position.

Table 22

Viewpoints on Church's Treatment of Groups

	Favor Change Percent of Views	Favor Status Quo Percent of Views		Number of Opinions
Women	56	44	100%	85
Minorities	89	11	100%	19
Laity	73	27	100%	15

Note: Based on sources expressing an explicit opinion on the Church's position.

Table 23

Viewpoints on Church and Dissent

	Approve Percent of Views	Disapprove Percent of Views		Number of Opinions
Church Response to Dissenters	33	67	100%	21
Church Response to Opinion Differences	25	75	100%	24

Note: Based on sources expressing an explicit opinion on the Church's position.

Table 24

Viewpoints on the Church Power Structure by Outlet

	Favor Change Percent of Views	Favor Status Quo Percent of Views		Number of Opinions
CBS	40	60	100%	10
Time	63	37	100%	32
Washington Post	66	34	100%	106
New York Times	65	35	100%	37
All Outlets	64	36	100%	185

Note: Based on sources expressing an explicit opinion on the Church's position.

Table 25

Viewpoints on Ecumenism by Source Type

	Support Percent of Views	Oppose Percent of Views		Number of Opinions
Church Hierarchy	78	22	100%	36
Priests and religious	100	0	100%	4
Laity	80	20	100%	5
All Others	62	38	100%	60
Overall	70	30	100%	105

Note: Based on sources expressing an explicit opinion on the Church's position.

Table 26

Viewpoints on Christian Unity

	Yes Percent of Views	No Percent of Views		Number of Opinion
Christian Unity Desirable	100	0	100%	21
Church is Obstacle	50	50	100%	24

Note: Based on sources expressing an explicit opinion on the Church's position.

Table 27

Viewpoints on Ecumenism by Era

	Support Percent of Views	Oppose Percent of Views		Number of Opinions
1960s	68	32	100%	40
1970s	75	25	100%	28
1980s	69	31	100%	36

Note: Based on sources expressing an explicit opinion on the Church's position.

Table 28

Viewpoints on Ecumenism by Outlet

	Support Percent of Views	Oppose Percent of Views		Number of Opinions
CBS	60	40	100%	5
Time	65	35	100%	17
Washington Post	67	33	100%	55
New York Times	78	22	100%	28
All Outlets	70	30	100%	105

Note: Based on sources expressing an explicit opinion on the Church's position.

Table 29

Viewpoints on Church Involvement in Politics by Era

	Appropriate Percent of Views	Not Appropriate Percent of Views		Number of Opinions
1960s	58	42	100%	19
1970s	55	45	100%	11
1980s	40	60	100%	15

Note: Based on sources expressing an explicit opinion on the Church's position.

Table 30

Viewpoints on Church Involvement in Politics by Outlet

	Appropriate Percent of Views	Not Appropriate Percent of Views		Number of Opinions
CBS	60	40	100%	5
Time	33	67	100%	3
Washington Post	50	50	100%	20
New York Times	53	47	100%	17
All Outlets	51	49	100%	45

Note: Based on sources expressing an explicit opinion on the Church's position.

Table 31

Viewpoints on Church Involvement in Politics by Source Type

	Appropriate Percent of Views	Not Appropriate Percent of Views		Number of Opinions
Church Hierarchy	100	0	100%	16
Priests and religious	75	25	100%	4
Laity	25	75	100%	4
All Others	14	86	100%	21
Overall	51	49	100%	45

Note: Based on sources expressing an explicit opinion on the Church's position.

Table 32

Viewpoints on Church Involvement in Politics

	Appropriate Percent of Views	Not Appropriate Percent of Views		Number of Opinions
War and Peace	83	17	100%	12
All Other Issues	39	61	100%	33

Note: Based on sources expressing an explicit opinion on the Church's position.

Table 33

Ideological Characterizations of the Church by Outlet

	Conservative Percent of Stories	Liberal Percent of Stories		Number of Stories
CBS	75	25	100%	24
Time	74	26	100%	81
New York Times	63	37	100%	80
Washington Post	53	47	100%	114
All Outlets	63	37	100%	299

Table 34
Ideological Characterizations of the Church by Era

	Conservative Percent of Stories	Liberal Percent of Stories		Number of Stories
1960s	59	41	100%	127
1970s	66	34	100%	77
1980s	65	35	100%	95

Table 35
Characterizations of Church Control by Outlet

	Oppressive Percent of Stories	Liberating Percent of Stories		Number of Stories
CBS	100	0	100%	5
Time	82	18	100%	39
Washington Post	91	9	100%	46
New York Times	76	24	100%	25
All Outlets	85	15	100%	115

Table 36
Characterizations of Church Control by Era

	Oppressive Percent of Stories	Liberating Percent of Stories		Number of Stories
1960s	76	24	100%	46
1970s	79	21	100%	29
1980s	100	0	100%	40

Table 37
Characterizations of the Relevance of the Church by Outlet

	Irrelevant Percent of Stories	Relevant Percent of Stories		Number of Stories
CBS	80	20	100%	5
Time	83	17	100%	18
Washington Post	59	41	100%	22
New York Times	58	42	100%	12
All Outlets	85	15	100%	57

Table 38

Characterizations of the Relevance of the Church by Era

	Irrelevant Percent of Characterizations	Relevant Percent of Characterizations		Number of Stories
1960s	66	34	100%	32
1970s	60	40	100%	10
1980s	80	20	100%	15

II. The Conference ✤

A Catholic Response to the Media

L. Brent Bozell III

L. BRENT BOZELL III is founder of the Media Research Center, Alexandria, Va., and Chairman of its board of directors. His work has been published in many periodicals and he has appeared frequently on television and radio.

WHILE MANY HAVE fought for years in the trenches to effect a change in media behavior, it was Drs. Robert Lichter and Stanley Rothman who first firmly placed the national press on the defensive with their famous study, *Media and Business Elites*. Published in 1981, it demolished the notion of the press as an apolitical observer of society by documenting the far-left personal persuasions of most journalists. The media, in response, maintained that they are "objective" in their coverage of news events, that personal beliefs are put on hold when the cameras start rolling.

Since 1981, however, dozens of studies on countless issues have demonstrated a definitive agenda in the press. These studies make up a complex quilt of empirical data which has shattered the canard that is the term "objective media." If one believes, as I do, that human nature makes pure objectivity impossible, and that the media are the microphone for ideas in the modern world, then the term "objective media" is an oxymoron. While most would agree that the press is biased, the media have long resisted any public scrutiny of their performance while demanding irrefutable evidence — curiously, a criterion not expected in their own work — before agreeing to address the charges.

We Catholics have long maintained that the national media have employed a sometimes curious, often purely negative, approach to matters related to the Church's teachings, her leaders, and her mission. The press, in response, has greeted complaints from Catholics with a universal yawn of indifference. Show us the evidence, they demand. Ten years after his first ground-breaking study, Dr. Lichter has done it again. Along with his wife, Dr. Linda Lichter, and fellow researcher Daniel Amundson, Bob Lichter has systematically proven the anti-Catholic bias in the national media. Their report, *Media Coverage of the Catholic Church*, provides Catholics with the intelligence needed to confront the press.

The signature of a Lichter-conducted study is the employment of the social-science method of content analysis. By employing the qualitative method of content analysis to determine thematic trends, and then supplementing that research with a quantitative analysis to study those data in numerical terms, a scientific picture emerges. The researchers chose one national network, CBS; one newsmagazine, *Time*; and two newspapers, *The Washington Post* and *The New York Times*. Each is representative of the medium in question; joined together they are representative of the media as a whole.

The authors broke down the analysis into three time periods (1964-68, 1974-78, and 1984-88) which enabled them to determine what currents of change, if any, were evident in media coverage. As will be noted shortly, this exercise provided a critical insight into the overall picture of anti-Catholic bias in the media.

By analyzing the media's coverage of the Catholic Church over a quarter of a century, the authors present a disturbing picture which neither responsible journalists nor supporters of the Church can ignore. The authors focused on four controversial themes which, by definition, reflect an agenda: sexual morality; Church authority and dissent; ecumenism and church-state relations; and descriptive language employed by the press.

Not surprisingly, the national media have advanced, aggressively, dissent from Church teachings on sexual morality. In the 1960s, during the era of Hans Küng and Charles Curran, this was the fifth most reported topic in the press. In the 1970s, it dropped to tenth, but in the 1980s it rocketed to third. Overall, the authors found that four out of every seven statements made about Church teachings were in opposition to those teachings, and that the level of antagonism has grown steadily in recent years. A case in point is abortion. In the 1960s, it was not an issue; in the 1970s it emerged, and opinion favored the Church's teachings; by the 1980s the pendulum of opinion statements had swung against the Church.

The second major area of controversy concerned the authority of the Catholic Church. Specifically, the media devoted tremendous coverage to the argument that the power of the Church should be decentralized. Issues cited included academic freedom of speech, women's rights, racism, and sexism. Statements in opposition to the Church's authority outweighed those supporting the Church by almost a 2-to-1 ratio; among non-Catholics, the level of opposition was almost universal at 91 percent to nine percent.

The third field of interest for the press centered on ecumenism and church-state relations. Interestingly, most statements dealing with Church efforts to build unity with other religions favored the concept; on the other hand, half of those same statements labeled the Church as the obstacle to that goal. On matters dealing with the Church's involvement in political affairs, the media provided overwhelmingly positive status to her anti-war stance (particularly during Vietnam), but were in fierce opposition on everything else. In the 1960s the media generally supported Church positions; in the 1970s negative comments outweighed positive ones by a factor of two-to-one; by the 1980s that figure had risen to a three-to-one ratio.

Finally, the authors looked at the language employed by the media to describe the Catholic Church. Throughout the three-decade period the Church was regularly labeled as conservative, but when characterizations of the relevance of the Church were tabulated, researchers found that in the 1960s, 66 percent described the Church as insignificant; by the 1980s that number had risen to an overwhelming 80 percent. Even more disturbing evidence of the growing hostility to the Church emerged when the researchers divided stories about the Church between the categories of "oppressive" and "liberating." In the 1960s, 76 percent of stories fell under the category of "oppressive"; in the 1970s the number had risen to 79 percent; in the 1980s, fully 100 percent of the stories studied cast the Roman Catholic Church in the "oppressive" classification.

Why the bias against the Catholic Church? The authors attempt two explanations. First, they re-explore the personal biases of reporters as documented in a previous work by the Lichters: only 12 percent of the media as a whole consider themselves Catholic while 86 percent of the media as a whole do not attend religious services regularly. Through interpolation one reaches the figure of an insignificant two percent for practicing Catholics, which is to say: Catholics who support the Church account for only two percent of the media as a whole. Moreover, the media personally oppose the Church on an entire gamut of issues, ranging from religious affiliation (50 percent have none); to abortion (90 percent support it); to homosexuality (76 percent disagree that "homosexuality is wrong"); to adultery (54 percent find it acceptable).

While the authors correctly state that this does not provide scientific evidence of bias in the stories filed by reporters, logic dictates otherwise. How can such personal and militant opposition to Church positions not color a reporter's story? Hypothetically, if a survey of reporters' views on Nazi Germany were to indicate that, say, 97 percent disapproved of the Holocaust, 93 percent disapproved of Hitler's imperialism, and 87 percent supported Allied efforts to defeat him, wouldn't it be realistic to assume that the media's coverage would be subjective and in opposition to Nazism? And wasn't that precisely the case?

Along with philosophical differences, the authors suggest a natural friction between the missions of the Church and journalism: "The Church provides information melded to interpretations based on doctrines it holds to be true and proper. . . . For the journalist, balancing opinions on an issue, the credibility of sources and concerns over legal formulas of fairness shape the presentation and analysis of information. These differing approaches inevitably lead to conflict between the two institutions. In assembling the news, the truth of Catholic teachings is opened to debate, just as the truths in a political speech are open to question."

But that does not excuse the media's performance either. If the press were exhibiting fairness and balance in its coverage of the Church there would be a certain continuity in its approach. In fact, this study proves just the opposite: over a period of 25 years the opposition to the Church has intensified to the point that today we can accuse the press of anti-Catholic bigotry.

Bigotry is a serious charge, to be sure. It denotes antagonism toward the Church and her mission and thus raises the accusation that there is a deliberate agenda against her.

Can such an allegation be supported? I think so. I certainly do not suggest all journalists are individually culpable: few are. But the refusal on the part of the media — so quick to expose bigotry in other fields — to denounce the bigotry that exists is an indictment of the institution as a whole.

As we enter the 1990s, the hostility toward the Catholic Church is reaching a fever pitch. Let's examine some specific examples, keeping in mind the overall analysis of the study results.

On May 4, 1990, NBC's Tom Brokaw covered the Pope's visit to Mexico and found "a country where there's a huge population problem. Many people say that problem is magnified by the Church's opposition to birth control. . . . Family planning experts say that ignorance and superstition play a big role in Mexico's population crisis . . . the Catholic Church has to share the blame."

On June 18, 1990, NBC's Katherine Couric covered Cardinal John O'Connor's statement that Catholic pro-abortion politicians might be excommunicated. After allowing for a quote from Cardinal O'Connor, Couric followed with five denunciations from five pro-abortion Catholic political leaders, including Governor Mario

Cuomo, Senator Daniel Moynihan, Representative Charles Rangel, former Representative Geraldine Ferraro, and Frances Kissling of Catholics for Free Choice. No Catholic pro-life views were entertained to defend Cardinal O'Connor, and Couric's opinion was obvious in her conclusion: "The Cardinal's warning has been questioned by others within the Church hierarchy, who have distanced themselves from his stand, and many Catholic lay people undoubtedly disagree."

On September 25, 1990, Deborah Norville interviewed ex-nuns Barbara Ferraro and Patricia Hussey, authors of a book attacking the Vatican's position on abortion. One softball question after another was offered up for the former nuns to hit out of the ballpark with anti-Catholic statements like "Repression is alive and well in the Roman Catholic Church." No opposing viewpoints. No confrontational questions to two women out to disgrace the Church through vicious attacks. Instead, this conclusion from the "objective" interviewer: "Yours is a story that so many of us have followed for so many years now, and it's a pleasure to have a chance to update how you are and what you've done with your lives. We wish you well."

The day before, in *Newsweek*, there appeared a story entitled "Ireland, AIDS, and the Church" The crisis? AIDS in Ireland. The culprit? You guessed it. The reason? "In the worldwide war against AIDS, education has been one of the few weapons that work. Irish AIDS activists, however, are coming up against deep-rooted denial and ignorance. Doctors who try to spread the word about safe sex face a formidable obstacle in the Roman Catholic Church. . ."

And, finally, this jewel from *Time* magazine just last month. In a story dealing with teenage sex and AIDS, Msgr. John Woolsey of New York was quoted championing abstinence, saying, "A huge campaign could work to stop kids from having sex. AIDS was caused in this country by promiscuity and casual sex. It is not traditional values that have brought us to where we are." *Time's* contempt for that position is evident in the very next sentence: "But AIDS activists and health-care workers have seen firsthand the devastation that ignorance can yield."

It is not just how the media interpret events or what the media consider to be newsworthy that should bother Catholics, it is what the media consider to be acceptable public discourse which is shocking. By presenting an argument as credible, the news media have the unique and awesome power to elevate an issue — no matter how heinous — to the level of permissible conversation. Such is the case with the news media's embrace of Hollywood's ferocious assault on the Roman Catholic Church.

When Hollywood released *The Last Temptation of Christ*, the news media greeted the firestorm from enraged Christians with amusement and indifference. More importantly, by giving the makers of this film equal footing with Christians, the media established as acceptable the public assault on Christianity and opened the floodgates for organized anti-Catholic bigotry.

The Media Research Center recently completed a year-long analysis of religious themes on prime-time television and found that, with the exception of one drama series, *thirtysomething*, not one show depicted Christianity in a favorable light. Instead, Christians in general and Catholics in particular were regularly depicted as ignorant, bigoted laughing stocks in comedy series and as hateful hypocritical abortion-clinic-bombing fanatics in drama shows and made-for-TV movies.

At a time when national surveys show that nine out of ten Americans hold strong religious beliefs, I ask you: Have you seen a single news story dedicated to Hollywood's assault on religion? (For the record, the day I penned these words, CNN ran a story on this very issue, and I applaud them for doing so.)

When PBS, at taxpayers' expense, recently aired *Tongues United*, a documentary glorifying black homosexuality through graphic pornographic images and dialogue, did anyone in the media find it newsworthy to cover the story from the perspective of a taxpayer-funded assault on Christian teachings? No.

Media mogul Ted Turner once called Christianity "a religion for losers" and pro-lifers "bozos [who] look like idiots." Last year he launched *Captain Planet and the Planeteers*, a morning cartoon series designed to teach his philosophy to children between the ages of three and eight. One episode called "The Population Bomb" glorified family planning and urged its young audience to practice birth control when they grow up. Did anyone in the news media consider it newsworthy that this form of brainwashing is a direct assault on the teachings of the Catholic Church? No.

Madonna recently told the gay magazine, *The Advocate*, "Catholicism is a really mean religion and it's incredibly hypocritical. How could I be supportive of it as an organized religion? I think [Jesus and Mary Magdalene] probably got it on." Did the news media consider it of interest that one of the world's best-known performers is actively slandering the Catholic Church? No.

And how about Amanda Donohoe, one of the stars of the Emmy award-winning *L.A. Law*? She portrays an active bisexual, and recently had a role in the movie *Lair of the White Worm*, in which her character spits on a crucifix. Asked by the entertainment magazine *Interview* how she felt playing these roles, Donohoe replied, "I'm an atheist, so it was actually a joy. Spitting on Christ was a great deal of fun."

I think of all the news reporters who dutifully reported

the racist bigotry of Dodger coach Al Campanis and sportscaster Jimmy the Greek, and wonder: Where are they now?

I think of all the reporters who dutifully reported the anti-semitic bigotry of Louis Farrakhan and Jesse Jackson and wonder: Where are they now?

More to the point: Where are the Catholics?

Virtually every segment of society recognizes the importance of the media, yet this somehow continues to escape Catholics. We sit back silently, witnessing the onslaught, unable or, worse, unwilling to respond. And I submit this is precisely why the Catholic Church has become such effortless target practice for her enemies and why anti-Catholic bigotry has become permissible behavior in the eyes of the anti-Catholic press.

In the last few years we have witnessed Cardinal O'Connor's almost single-handed effort to stop the media's hostility to the Church and her values; those of us who have done nothing to help him should feel real shame. We have also observed the commitment of the Knights of Columbus to correct this problem, and while I am filled with admiration and gratitude for their leadership, I question why we believe it necessary to hire, to the tune of several million dollars, a high-powered Washington, D.C., public relations firm to do our bidding.

It is time for Catholics — lay Catholics — to stand up and be counted. To recognize that our Church is under attack in a most deliberate attempt to discredit and ultimately destroy her. To expose and denounce the bigotry aimed against us through and by the national media. Yes, Church leaders must take a stronger stand, and I earnestly pray some will follow in the valiant footsteps of Cardinal O'Connor in denouncing the discrimination against the Church.

But much more must be done. Lay Catholic organizations must individually and collectively dedicate themselves to the fight against the bias in the media by devoting the necessary resources and energy to making this a top priority on their agendas. The spokesmen must actively present themselves to the media to denounce any and all efforts to discredit the Church through bigotry. Catholic periodicals, like *The Wanderer*, *Twin Circle*, etc., should regularly and diligently monitor and expose those in the press who are systematically using the "news" media to distort current events in order to discredit the Church. Catholics in a position of influence — elected officials at every level of government, political activists, even members of the media — must use their stations as pulpits from which to challenge the bigots.

It is time for a Catholic response. We must accept the challenge this sobering study offers us. Never in history has our Church been threatened in such a manner. It will not be easy to confront a multi-billion dollar enterprise with the power to change our country's cultural landscape. But I don't suggest we confront it. I suggest we capture it.

Response to L. Brent Bozell III

By The Honorable Frank Shakespeare

FRANK SHAKESPEARE is former Senior Vice President of the CBS-TV network, former President of CBS-TV Services, and former President of RKO General, Inc. He has served as Director of the United States Information Agency, United States Ambassador to Portugal and to the Holy See, Chairman of Radio Free Europe / Radio Liberty, and Chairman of the Heritage Foundation.

I THINK BRENT Bozell's articulation of the Lichter study in its detail speaks for itself. But he made an observation, in the course of his dissertation, about what is acceptable public discourse in our country, and I want to develop that theme in an historical sense. I propose to do that by quoting the words of four Presidents of the United States.

I choose Presidents because under our special form of government, where a President is both king and prime minister, he becomes the voice of the society. What Presidents feel free to say, how they feel free to speak, is a very deep illustration of the parameters of acceptable public discourse.

To start, let me go back to the middle of the nineteenth century and quote Lincoln. Perhaps the greatest speech given by a President in the history of the United States — this is of course a very subjective interpretation — is Lincoln's Second Inaugural. At the time, the Civil War was winding down. Lincoln, as the President, was speaking to his fellow-citizens about how, in his view, they should think of the war which had ravaged, and was still ravaging, the country. Here are those extraordinary words which we all have read and heard so many times:

> Fondly do we hope, and fervently do we pray, that this mighty scourge of war may speedily pass away. Yet if God wills that it continue until all the wealth piled by the bondsman's two hundred and fifty years of unrequited toil shall be sunk, and until every drop of blood drawn with the lash shall be paid by another drawn with the sword, as was said three thousand years ago, still it must be said, "The judgments of the Lord are true and righteous altogether."

What was Lincoln saying? That slavery was basically a sin, and that man does not get away with it, and that the wrath of a righteous God can make itself felt — and perhaps in the Civil War *had* made itself felt. That was a profoundly Christian exposition. No sermon in church could have been clearer. Clearly, at that time, Lincoln understood himself to be a Christian leader addressing a Christian people.

Now skip from the middle of the nineteenth century to the middle of the twentieth century: to 1939, when World War II was looming on the horizon and the President was Franklin Roosevelt. Roosevelt wanted eyes and ears in a special place, the Vatican, but for political reasons it was very difficult — impossible, really —to establish an embassy. So he came up with the President's "Personal Representative" to the Vatican, a prominent Episcopalian, Myron Taylor, whom he used as a channel for formal and official letters between the chief of state of the Vatican, Pius XII, and the chief of state of our country.

I want to quote from just a few of Roosevelt's letters. These were not private letters; they were formal letters of the President to a foreign chief of state. Here is Roosevelt in December 1939, speaking of the turmoil of the world at the beginning of World War II:

> I take heart in remembering that in a similar time Isaiah first prophesied the birth of Christ. Then, several centuries before his coming, the condition of the world was not unlike that which we see today. Then, as now, a conflagration had been set. But in that very moment a spiritual rebirth was foreseen. I believe that while statesmen are considering a new order of things, it is even now being built silently but inevitably in the hearts of the masses, whose voices are not heard but whose common faith will write the final history of our time. They know that unless there is a belief in some guiding principle, and some trust in a divine plan, nations are without light, and people perish.

Soon the war is coming very close to the United States and ravaging Europe. Here is Roosevelt to Pius in March of 1941:

> Only when the principles of Christianity are established can that peace which we so ardently desire be found.

Again, Roosevelt, in a formal letter of the President, in September, 1941:

> We desire that a firm basis for the lasting concord between men and nations, founded on the principles of Christianity, again be established.

The war concludes. Roosevelt dies in April of 1945. Harry Truman, inexperienced, becomes President and faces the traumatic problem of trying to put the world together. Here is Truman to Pius, a formal letter in 1946:

> Although hostilities have ceased, peace has not yet been achieved. We must employ every resource at our command to bring an enduring

peace. And no peace can be permanent which is not based on Christian principles.

A year later — 1947. Now trouble with the Soviet Union is on the horizon. Truman to Pius:

> As the chosen leader of the people of the United States, I pledge full faith to work for an enduring peace. And enduring peace can be built only upon Christian principle. To such a consummation we dedicate all our resources, both spiritual and material, remembering always that except the Lord build the house, they labor in vain who build it. Your Holiness, this is a Christian nation. As a Christian nation, our earnest desire is to work with men of good will everywhere to banish war and the causes of war from the world, whose Creator desired that men should live together in peace, good will, and mutual trust.

And here is Truman again, in 1948. The Soviet threat is looming, and Truman, in this formal letter as President, less than 50 years ago, makes clear his understanding of the deepest philosophical principle of what was then United States foreign policy.

> The years immediately behind us have been fraught with difficulties. Although hostilities came to an end, our hopes for an enduring peace have been deferred. But we do not despair. Rather, in a spirit of rededication, should we renew our labors to achieve the peace of Christ in a world too long divided by enmity, jealousy, and ill-will. This nation holds out the hand of fellowship to all who would seek world unity under God, the Lord and Father of us all. We cannot, God forbid that we ever could, accept the teaching that religion is unnecessary, that Christianity is untrue.

That was the President fifty years ago.

Now, every man and woman in this room knows what would happen in this country if a President of the United States today, in official documents, used the phraseology and the substance of Roosevelt and Truman. Neither Roosevelt, who I think was an Episcopalian, nor Truman, who I think was a Methodist, had a reputation of being overtly, deeply religious, as for example Jimmy Carter was. I cite Roosevelt and Truman merely as evidence of how far we have moved, judged by what is today acceptable public reference.

How far have we come? Several years ago a President referred to a brutal, cruel, dehumanizing, tyrannical, multinational state as an "evil empire." We all know what happened. There could be no concern about the word "empire," since this was self-evidently an empire: Russians were ruling other people — Estonians, Latvians, Lithuanians, Georgians, and Armenians — who did not want to be ruled by the Russians. It was an empire in the same sense as the British Empire or the German Empire, or whatever. There could be no concern with "empire."

The concern was with the word "evil." Did it have to do with an indelicate reference to a sensitive international situation, a reference that might be destabilizing? Or was it perhaps that the use of the word "evil" by a President brought into play an archaic concept, a spiritual concept, deemed no longer suitable or appropriate in an enlightened, rational, secular society?

Four Presidents — Lincoln, Roosevelt, Truman, Reagan. They give us an idea of the change in our country in what is acceptable discourse by the leading voice of the United States, our king-prime minister.

Now I wish to make a second point, on which I shall close. I think that, as Brent Bozell remarked, the media are truly skeptical about religion, for whatever reasons, and probably because their own views stem from the Enlightenment and from rationalism. But in this country, if you are skeptical about religion, you focus your attention on Christianity, because that is the core of religion here. And if you focus on Christianity today, you focus on Catholicism, because of what is happening.

What do I mean by that? Part of the reason for the recent, rather intensive, hostile focus on Catholicism may be tradition. Anti-Catholicism is the anti-Semitism of intellectuals; we have all heard that for many years, and it is part of the tradition. But the focus today may also be a compliment, reflecting the reality of the spiritual forces at play.

Churchill had a buddy in the 1930s. His name was [Alfred] Duff Cooper. He was a very famous British diplomat, ambassador to France among other things, and also a great man for witticisms. One of his most famous was this: "For the British, there are only two kinds of religion, the Roman Catholic, which is wrong, and the rest, which don't matter."

Today as we look at our country, there is certain evidence — I am not a theologian, but it is simply self-evident — that doctrine is weakening. There was never an officially established church in the United States, of course, yet in the societal sense — the church of the elite, the governing class if you will — it was the Episcopal Church. It is very clear today that in theological terms the Episcopal Church is all over the lot. It does not appear to have a theological, doctrinal core any more. As for Judaism, although I am not really familiar with it, it seems to be the case that a substantial number, maybe even a majority, of Jews in the United States think of it perhaps as an ethnic and cultural reality rather than a theological reality. That is to say that many of them in their own view are agnostic, possibly even atheistic. Similar things are occurring in many other churches of the United States.

But the Catholic Church is becoming ever stronger, formally, on doctrine. That stems from Karol Wojtyla, the Polish Pope; it stems often from ferment within the Church, and the need to reassert principles in a strong way; it stems from [Cardinal Josef] Ratzinger, who is an extraordinarily brilliant man, and strong; it stems from many of the new cardinals in the United States — [Bernard] Law in Boston, [John] O'Connor in New York, [Anthony] Bevilacqua in Philadelphia, [James] Hickey in Washington, [Roger] Mahony in Los Angeles. So that, while this doctrinal, theological split and diminishing of other churches is occurring, in the Catholic Church there is a reaffirmation of doctrinal principles.

Also, there are the sheer numbers to help explain why there should be this sort of focus on anti-Catholicism now. Twenty-five percent, more or less, of the people of the United States are Catholic. This is by far the largest religious body in the country. But because Catholics tend to vote and others sometimes tend not to vote, in an average election the Catholic vote is likely to be as much as one third. Those are very, very big numbers. Much of the anti-Catholic ferment may stem from an instinctive awareness of the advance of the Catholic Church.

The Secular Character of Our Press

By Richard Harwood

RICHARD HARWOOD, at the time of this conference, had been with The Washington Post for over 25 years and was the paper's ombudsman; now he is a columnist. A former editor of The Times of Trenton, N.J., he is the author, co-author or editor of several books, including a biography of Lyndon Johnson and a collection of essays on journalism.

I AM GOING to speak about the history of the secular press. But first I want to make a point about some of the remarks that have been made here and that will be made, I think, and also about some of the interpretations of the Lichter study. It is that neither the Church nor the media are monolithic institutions.

A gentleman here corrected the percentage of Catholics in the media. The Lichter characterization of the religious affiliations of journalists referred only to four or five institutions. Among American newspapers in general, the percentages of people affiliated with various denominations very accurately replicate the society as a whole. Between 25 and 30 percent of American journalists are Catholic. I do not dispute the local figures. I want to make the point, however, that the media are not monolithic.

My second point is that even in the Lichter study you will find that the treatment of various issues varies among these institutions. Read it carefully, and that will help.

In any event, it is my view that the secular character of the American press — and it certainly has a secular character — was pretty well fixed by its history. Our newspapers evolved in a repressive theocratic culture in which the penalty for heresy or dissent might be death. Printing presses were licensed by authorities with the power to arbitrarily grant or revoke the privilege. Printers and authors were subject to both censorship and prosecutions under four sweeping categories of libel which are sometimes called "word crimes," a category of offense that is enjoying a rebirth on some university campuses today.

These Colonial crimes included libels defamatory of personal or professional reputation, libels defamatory of public officials and institutions, obscene and immoral libels defamatory of public standards of morality and libels of blasphemy. The blasphemy libel was rationalized in 1676 by Lord Hale of the King's Court: "Christianity being parcel of the laws of England, therefore to reproach the Christian religion is to speak in subversion of the law." Lord Mansfield, also of the King's Court, elaborated on that theme in 1767: "The eternal principles of natural religion are part of the common law; the essential principles of revealed religion are part of the common law; so that any person reviling, subventing or ridiculing them may be prosecuted at common law."

The adoption of the First Amendment to our Constitution did not wipe the slate clean on these matters. Well into the nineteenth century prosecutions for blasphemy continued to be brought under various state and local statutes. So it was obviously safer and less troublesome for editors to ignore religion than to plunge into troubled sectarian waters.

Another factor in this secular evolution was the commercial marketplace itself. Newspapers in the early nineteenth century began to wean themselves from financial dependence on political sponsorship or patronage. To achieve that purpose they needed a mass audience and advertising support. Because of the sectarian diversity of the audience, it was expedient not to give offense. So religion generally was ignored or handled as it is often handled today on the Saturday church page: innocuous announcements interspersed among paid advertisements for church services and revival meetings. "Such an approach," a report from the Religious News Service has noted, "did not even necessitate a religion reporter per se. Copy could be produced literally by anyone, because religion did not warrant specialist attention."

Partly as a result of this neglect, the religious press in America flourished in the nineteenth century. Presbyterians, Baptists, Catholics, Methodists, Congregationalists, Jews and Swedenborgians, Spiritualists, and sects of every description got into the publishing business: newspapers, magazines, collections of sermons, Bibles, children's material, and evangelistic pamphlets in many languages and dialects. By 1860 nearly 300 religious newspapers were being published with an annual press run of about 100 million copies.

Many efforts to establish dailies and attract ecumenical audiences were made, but they proved to be commercially unfeasible. Today only three daily newspapers with religious sponsors are published in the United States — the *Christian Science Monitor*, *Salt Lake Deseret News*, and the *Washington Times*. The Salt Lake paper may operate without direct subsidies. But both the *Monitor* and *Times* are heavily dependent on the financial support of their sponsors. Various religious periodicals, sponsored by local denominations and parishes, are presently found in virtually every state, but they circulate in limited numbers.

The message to the secular press from these unsatisfactory ventures was that there is no great market for such material; it validated their inattention to religious affairs in a society drenched in secular thought propagated through our educational system, literature, art, television, films, and music.

Finally, as Robert Lichter has suggested, the secular character of our newspapers is not totally divorced from the interests or character of the people who produce them. American journalists have roughly the same religious attachments as other Americans. But among the "media elite" Lichter found that religious attachments tend to be weak. That is true in my own case and is consistent with my impression of my colleagues. We were educated in secular institutions, are quite sensitive to changing fashions in secular intellectual thought and to the pseudo-secularism preached in many pulpits.

It follows, I think, that encounters between the Church and this "elite" or "prestige" press do not often occur in a religious setting — the confessional box, for example. They ordinarily occur, instead, in a secular context which very often is a political arena, a familiar ground for religionists in the United States.

Their involvement in secular affairs began here in the seventeenth century and continued through the Revolutionary War. In the years leading up to the Civil War, the religious press played an important role in abolitionist affairs. Protestant preachers whipped up sentiment for the war with Spain in 1898. In subsequent years, pornography, alcohol, dancing, card playing, and other secular pursuits engaged the attention of millions of Christians. More recently they have involved themselves in issues of war and peace, abortion, sexual behavior, economic justice, dissent, heresy, distant revolutions and uprisings, American foreign policy, tax policies, and labor disputes. Priests, preachers, nuns, and laymen in great numbers have, so to speak, come out of the cloister and into the streets. Some of them have gone off to various jails and prisons, and their activities, understandably, have drawn considerable media attention.

What I am trying to describe is a great intersection of the doctrinal affairs of the Catholic Church and the political affairs of this secular society. When we talk about abortion, we are not merely talking about matters of faith or doctrine. We are talking about laws, which are enacted by political bodies. The naming of people to the Supreme Court presumably is a secular matter, but it has become involved in these doctrinal disputes.

One result of the intrusion of religious bodies and individuals into secular affairs — a result involving not only the Catholic Church but all the churches — has not always been flattering to the participants. It is that familiarity can bring with it demystification, a loss of deference, and an erosion of institutional standing.

It should surprise none of us, given our history, that a secular press should bring secular rather than theological attitudes to the coverage of all these issues, whether it is abortion or sexual morality or the institutional conflict which has been described as dissension within the Catholic Church. Mr. Shakespeare described it very well.

But the media are accused of, in effect, creating the popular culture. I do not believe that. We reflect the culture. We claim to mirror it, but we are usually behind the curve. But we do reflect it — the values expressed in newspapers do reflect this popular culture. One reason people who disagree with a paper like the *Post* or the *Times* get so outraged is that they think the paper is brainwashing people and influencing society. But the reality is as a Kentucky politician said to another politician: "Sir, your influence is tissue-paper thin, I say, tissue-paper thin." I think *our* influence is tissue-paper thin. Nonetheless we do reflect this popular culture.

The Lichter report tells us that "on most controversies involving Catholic teachings, the Church came out on the losing side of the issue debate reported in the media." The method here is to count up the people quoted in a particular story, and come up with a percentage — three out of five, or whatever the numbers are — for or against a particular position. The study found that sources supporting the Church were in the minority on a broad range of debates that involve sexual morality and Church authority. That would include birth control, clerical celibacy, the role of women and minorities, internal dissent, etc. You are familiar with all those things.

I do not challenge the statistical findings. I think that Bob Lichter and his people are excellent — accurate and reliable researchers. But I wonder at the significance of some of these numbers. Suppose those quoted on the issue of birth control divided 70 percent to 30 percent. I think that reflects the attitude of the American people. I do not see anything loaded there. And I think this is true on many of these issues: you cannot give the whole picture through these statistical devices.

Anyway, the study "found that members of the hierarchy were heavily cited [in major stories]; official teachings were frequently presented, most often without refutation by critics; on some issues the Church's teaching was endorsed by a majority of sources whose opinions were printed or broadcast. This ranged from abortion and homosexuality to ecumenism and questions of war and peace."

One reason for the disparity in the numbers is, as I said before, that the position of the Church on many of these issues is a minority position among Americans in general, and quite possibly among American Catholics as well. I think the people who ignore the teachings on birth control probably far exceed those who observe them. Not only in the United States, but in such countries as France, and even in places such as Italy, there is great opposition. The teachings on contraception, in my view, really have no intellectual standing in our society outside the Church, and perhaps with a minority within the Church. Possibly that could be said of other issues. I do not have numbers.

But as journalists we are under no obligation to give superior weight or credence to an institutional declaration of the Pope or the cardinals or whatever. We are under no obligation to give more weight to that than to a declaration by the President or the Speaker of the House, as against opposing positions. In much of the coverage, Bob Lichter found that we relied very, very heavily on Catholic sources on issues involving the Church. I calculated — Bob can correct this — that about 70 percent of the sources on Church positions, whether they were pro or con, were Catholic sources.

One view of these things is that Church issues are internal matters best resolved internally, and maybe the press ought to stay out of some of these things. But I think that is naive in an open society such as ours — a society in which secular and religious affairs, as I indicated, have become inseparable.

Richard Brookheiser, in an essay for *Time* magazine, has written that, "The Protestant churches seem obsessed with sex these days . . . [and] the terms of [the] discussion are revolutionary — not Why do men sin? but Why shouldn't they party? Traditional strictures against homosexuality, pre-marital sex (once called fornication), even adultery, are up for theological debate. . . .

"Roman Catholics have caught the bug, too. As in so many areas, liberal American Catholics find themselves playing catch-up with their Protestant soul mates. . . .

"The obvious secular explanation for this hubbub is that America's churches are internalizing the mores of a developed society . . . [But] what we are witnessing is in fact a clash between two earnest and articulated theological impulses. Traditionalists and innovators disagree about sex because they disagree about the universe and about God."

Rebellion against arbitrary authority and against the traditional social role of women in both secular and religious affairs is occurring as well. I refer to the Religious News Service study: The story of religion in America is starting to resemble other stories, and can be covered by the conventions applied to other stories. It has come to resemble a great political story. It has begun to have high-profile scandals, and all the rest. It is becoming less of an institutional story which can be handled by covering established bodies and their actions. Religion, this study said, is becoming more diverse and privatized, and is finding its way into the news in new and different ways and places.

I think that is what we are seeing today in our newspapers and in the other media. There is no question whatever that these media are secular institutions. There is no question that secular thought is the preferred body of thought within the media. But, as I said, we should not be surprised at that, because these media mirror the concerns and attitudes of the popular culture. I think that is not going to change; and if Bob Lichter comes back a few years from now and does a similar study, he is going to get the same results.

Response to Richard Harwood

Robert Royal

ROBERT ROYAL is Vice President for Research at the Ethics and Public Policy Center, Washington. He has taught at Brown University, Rhode Island College, and the Catholic University of America, and has contributed articles and reviews to many periodicals.

I HAVE ADMIRED Richard Harwood for a long time and for several reasons. Those of us who have the benefit of private sacramental confession know that in spite of the pain of having to tell someone the truth, relief usually follows. But poor Richard Harwood has to confess in public, without much hope of a forgiving listener, and not only confess his own sins, but those of his colleagues who, as in any large group, may not always be of the most lovable sort. I imagine he gets little relief from the often very fine confessions and analyses he carries out as ombudsman for *The Washington Post*.

Nevertheless, in spite of all my admiration for him, his history of newspaper coverage of religion strikes me as a reasonably good explanation, but hardly an excuse. However much at times reading *The Washington Post* I have lamented the demise of the anti-blasphemy laws — to say nothing of the demise of a mere grudging respect toward the Catholic Church — his argument that the press is wary of religious controversies because of such laws centuries ago, or even in the last century, strikes me as a stale defense. If in his heyday Ben Bradlee, to take a now inactive and neutral *corpus vile*, could have been threatened with public dunking for blasphemy — a picturesque thought — maybe worry over theological controversies would have been understandable. But Ben Bradlee was about as likely to have been publicly dunked for blasphemy as he was to be ridden out of town on a rail for political controversy.

I also feel obliged to point out that the problem with most coverage of the Catholic Church is not that it brings secular rather than theological attitudes to the coverage of public issues, but that it brings unconscious theological prejudices to those issues without realizing it. If, as it has recently, *The Washington Post* can examine, with the thoroughness and subtlety of a medieval metaphysician, the various facets of the question of whether the selection of the latest Miss America was a beauty pageant or a scholarship contest, then is it too much to ask that religious issues be treated with some degree of knowledge and intellectual rigor, or with a proper wariness that avoidable biases should not be introduced?

Let me give you a concrete example of what I mean. As the Lichter study shows scientifically and all of us know instinctively, many of the stories in the press about the Catholic Church have to do with questions of power and authority within the institution. The received image of the Church among most secular intellectuals, if that term is appropriate for journalists, is of an authoritarian hierarchy that stifles the spontaneous spirituality and concrete morality of the people.

As a different form of range-finding, however, let me draw your attention to a comparison. When the national committee of the NAACP voted in August to oppose the nomination of Clarence Thomas to the Supreme Court, a local NAACP chapter in Compton, California, was already on record supporting him. The national committee sent the local committee a message outlining the following alternatives:

1. The local could rescind the endorsement; or,
2. The members of the local could resign.

The news stories about this conflict played it straight down the middle, with no commentaries about motives, legitimacies, or authoritarianism. And for all I know, the national NAACP was within its corporate rights in issuing the ultimatum.

But it might be edifying to think about what the media coverage would have looked like had the Pope issued a similarly sharp set of instructions about how to resolve an issue. I ought to say that, unlike some of my fellow Catholics, I don't think the Church ought to be so absolute very often, except in cases of grave public scandal or serious leading astray of God's people: a few such cases have emerged in the United States in recent years and I think the Vatican has been right to act when it did. But it illuminates our discussion here to notice that charges of authoritarianism and insensitivity get inhibited in the one case by media respect for the NAACP. In the Catholic case, no such respect would be forthcoming. A professional journalist, it seems to me, would be bothered by that fact.

Furthermore, religious prejudices — not only the incomprehension of the Catholic Church — have widely distorted the news about religious bodies. It is understandable that many religious stories deal with Church debates over homosexuality, or women priests, or a celibate clergy. But most of the people doing the reporting have the impression that because these issues are important to journalists, they are important to the people in the pews. As every competent survey has shown, however, people in the pews are not leaving the old Protestant mainline churches because the Methodists, or Presbyterians, or Episcopalians are too demanding. The usual journalistic paradigm is that people feel oppressed —as the journalist himself or herself might — at being told what to do, and are being driven out by an insensitive church bureaucracy. All the surveys, however, show that the constantly liberalizing oldline churches are declining while the more conservative, even fundamentalist, groups of all denominations are growing. I am not particularly a fan of fundamentalism of any sort, but these are the facts about current religious dynamics in the United States.

Another distortion of the news: reading the secular press, you would never have the impression that the best selling books in the United States are religious books. Some of these, though far from all, are not of very high quality; but if the best seller lists can allow Sidney Sheldon and Jackie Collins in the fiction column, they should be able to show some religious titles in the non-fiction column.

To be fair to the main news outlets, papers like the *Post* do a reasonably good job of covering the Catholic Church when their attention — I mean the full attention of the editors — is engaged. The *Post*'s coverage of the Reverend George Stallings, for example, I would judge not entirely bad. Investigative reporters looked hard into the allegations of sexual activity with altar boys; Stallings' egoism and demagoguery came through fairly clearly; and the financial improprieties were duly reported. I don't think enough space was given to Cardinal Hickey's role in helping George Stallings, from his time in the seminary until the time of the controversy (Hickey was roughly for Stallings what the Georgia Catholic nuns were for Clarence Thomas). Yet the coverage was not wholly bad. To me, this just shows that when the editors want to get serious about investigating and reporting on a story in some sense religious, they can do it right.

Yet they can also do quite poorly when their attention is not engaged. I hope the example I'm about to use will not be considered trivial in the present context, but I use it because I know all the principals personally.

When I read stories about the Catholic Church, I'm often reminded of George Orwell's astonishment when he returned from the Spanish Civil War. He found that in England, entire series of analytical articles were written pro and con about news stories from Spain reporting events which, he knew from direct experience, had never occurred. Many stories about the Church are like that.

The example I'd like to use is the story that appeared recently in the *Post* about a girl who was not allowed to receive her diploma from the altar of the church at graduation from a Catholic school because the nuns thought she was improperly dressed. As I say, I know the people involved in this incident, and, given the personalities, there was plenty of blame to go around. But the way in which the story was pursued by the reporter showed sheer laziness. The mother's account, defending the daughter and the dress, was amply presented. Little reply from the school. In the closing paragraphs, the suggestion was even made without further follow up that racism had something to do with it.

Given the wild ethnic makeup of the school in question, this is particularly laughable. (I never know ahead of time the race, or even the continent of origin, of many of the classmates my kids have sleeping over at the house.) This is a discrete incident, but when lack of attention of this sort occurs again and again, and the gaps left by poor reporting are filled in largely by a kind of native American antipathy to Catholicism mixed with current liberal biases, journalists should not be surprised that Catholics are angry at their reporting.

Reporters are using theological categories all the time in their stories about the Catholic Church — unconsciously for the most part — and they should, if they are on this particular beat, be encouraged to leave their own prejudices out of the news stories as much as their counterparts on the political beat.

Let's come to specifics. The point where the Catholic shoe pinches is largely over sexual issues. Few news stories tell the exciting details of the latest theological debates over the human and divine natures of Christ. Rarely, to my knowledge, has a story surfaced in the *Post* about the delicate and equally exciting new thinking about biblical hermeneutics. By the time a story enters the general media, it usually comes out talking about whether a female priest can represent a male Christ, whether God can be called father, or whether anybody, particularly anybody ordained, can tell anybody else it is wrong to have sex or to abort a baby.

While I appreciate Richard Harwood's candor in saying that the Church's position on many of these issues is a minority position, perhaps even among Catholics, I'm afraid this too is not an excuse. We are in a moment of heightened sensitivities to all sorts of minority positions. Mr. Harwood would not dream of telling an African-American who found some phrases subtly racist that he should understand the history of American journalism and the predominantly white make-up of current society and intellectual culture. Such arguments would be evidence of the prejudice being indicted.

Multiculturalism either means allowing a place for the Church that has had the longest and most profound influence on our culture, or it really means something other than what is says. No one is saying that religious reporters have to agree with the Church, merely that they should be cautious whom they cite, and how, in controversies. A. E. Housman once parodied the biblical hermeneutics of his time by using them to prove that Gladstone was a Sun Myth. Many of the religious experts quoted in secular stories may, in the not-so-long run, prove to have about as much substance as Housman's targets.

In conclusion, let me just say that I read with no end of amusement the general mental laziness of the typical media commentator on the Church. The institution is approaching its 2,000th birthday, and, if truth be told, a lot can happen in 2,000 years. Yet the usual news story implies that things started okay with Jesus, quickly degenerated with Paul into homophobia and general uptightness, then slid into a long stretch of Dark Ages, Crusades, and, of course, the Inquisition. Since Vatican II a couple of priests, a bishop here and there, have understood something —occasionally a learned pressman might remember that Francis of Assisi had redeeming moments — something to do with environmentalism and animal rights. But overall, in this mental image there's been little good in this nearly billion-member monstrosity that somehow manages to limp on from age to age, civilization to civilization.

Then, of course there was Galileo. Today, anybody who stands up against the Church is compared with Galileo (the opponents like Hitler and Stalin perhaps excepted). I hope this is not uncharitable, but these comparisons remind me of the Austrian journalist Karl Kraus's observation that in the modern world "every stink that fights the ventilator thinks it is Don Quixote."

If I could get one message about Catholicism across to the men and women who bring me most of my news about the world, it would be this. Galileo was wrongly condemned, even by Catholic standards, for his scientific views. There were also some theological issues involved in the case that were not as straightforward, but little matter now about such obscure events — we all know now that he was right about the science. But my advice to the journalists is this simple logical truth: Just because Galileo stood up to the Church and was wrongly censured for speaking the truth, not everyone who says he is speaking the truth in spite of the Church is Galileo.

A Fine Study: But How Much Does It Matter?

Michael J. Robinson

MICHAEL J. ROBINSON is Associate Professor of Government at Georgetown University, Washington, D.C., and also has taught at Ohio State University, the University of Michigan, and the University of Virginia. He is published widely on the subject of mass media and American politics.

I AM NOT a practicing Catholic. In fact, I am not a Catholic. But for the last 20 years I have been a practicing content analyst. So, as a practicing content analyst, I can with some credentials come before you and offer an assessment of *Media Coverage of the Catholic Church*. This is the most recent in a long list of content analytic studies done by the Center for Media and Public Affairs — CMPA as it is known in Washington, probably the single most visible "content analysis" workshop in America.

Let me get right to my point. I think CMPA's research, presented in this volume, is, as is typical with CMPA, scholarly, objective, and valid. I do not much doubt CMPA's major conclusion about the press coverage, per se, of the Church these last 25 years: In short, that "during the post-Vatican II era . . . the Church [is] found on the losing side of the battle of ideas, an institution depicted as conservative, oppressive, and out of touch."

And I am even a bit more persuaded by CMPA's less sweeping conclusion as it appears in the executive summary: That "on most controversies involving Catholic teachings, the Church came out on the losing side of the issue debate reported in the media." Specifically, "sources *supporting* (italics mine) the Church were in the minority on the broad range of debates involving sexual morality and Church authority." In the main, I accept these conclusions as empirical truth.

Now for the not so good news — as I see it — about all this "bad news" that CMPA uncovered in its research about the Church and the News Media.

I could start with those few minor methodological problems that I see here. But I shall hold off on those until later, not merely because they *are* minor problems, but also because I want to get to the big stuff early on. And just as I wanted to get to my first point as quickly as possible — that I think CMPA is right, in large part, about news content — I want just as much to get to my next biggest point: I think the report makes some mistakes in its assumptions about the meaning of all this content analysis for the Church.

My biggest problem has to do with the stated assumptions in the very first line of the report, something of a throwaway line that Lichter, Amundson and Lichter give to us: "[The] public image of social groups and institutions depends *heavily* on their portrayal in the news media" (italics mine).

That is an assumption with which I am in disagreement. We have had people point out here today that the press is secular and the country is religious, that the press goes one way and the country goes another. So, this is an assumption to be tested. A few years ago, when I was working on the same floor of the George Washington University library with the Lichters, I discovered by implication while doing my own content research, that their opening line in this report is not necessarily accurate.

Specifically, I found back in 1984 that on network news there was *nine times* as much "bad press" about the Reagan-Bush ticket in that campaign as about Mondale-Ferraro. I guess most of you remember that the public did not see things that way; Reagan-Bush carried 49 states. If one discovers, as I did, that the press can be just awful in the way it treats a ticket (or an institution), and then discovers that the bad press has not had much effect, one becomes less willing to accept that assumption that the public "depends heavily" on the news media for formulating its opinions.

Or take the North case. The press was generally critical toward Oliver North. Certainly the political establishment on the Hill was critical of North. Yet this week I was told, by a person who insists on anonymity, that the leadership of the Democratic Party realized the more critical they became of North, the more supportive the country became. He also told me that in the Bork case exactly the same thing happened: Surveys conducted day to day showed that, despite the press and the elite pummeling by the Democrats in the Senate, Judge Robert Bork's reputation with the American people went up day by day.

If, too, you imagine that it is always conservatives who get bad press while the country ignores it, consider Teddy Kennedy. Senator Kennedy has been getting a lot of negative press. But the last survey I saw showed that 65 percent still planned to vote for him in the state of Massachusetts in his next Senate race, although there has been some slippage there.

So, I am asking the three scholars this morning not so

much about their coding rules or their sampling frames (although I do have some problem with the "two-to-one" rule and the decision to exclude the Lefebvre controversy from this analysis). Instead I ask about the implications of their findings. My guess is that despite the seriousness of this content analysis and its valid content findings, the numbers revealed herein may not matter very much. Not in the real world of real effects. I say so for three reasons.

First, the coverage of the Church in the news media may not matter very much because the data in this study show that the bias against the Church is not all that bad. Nothing that CMPA uncovers supports the outrageous conclusion by Michael Schwartz, cited by CMPA, that the American media portray Catholicism "as ridiculous or cruel or repressive." And that "the mass media image of Catholics is only slightly better than that of Nazis!"

Fortunately — very fortunately — CMPA quotes Mr. Schwartz, but CMPA never tells us that he is correct. Schwartz most certainly is wrong, and CMPA's own data lead one to believe that.

Let us take a quick look at how biased the news coverage actually is in this study. According to CMPA, 85 percent of the stories that dealt with the dimension of "control" by the Church implied that the Church was "oppressive" as opposed to "liberating" (15 percent). For CBS the figures were 100 percent "oppressive" and zero percent "liberating." That suggests negative bias, all right, but only five stories on CBS analyzed in this study dealt with control — five stories out of 231 stories, about two percent of the total.

It seems to me that many of the appendicized tables in *Media Coverage of the Catholic Church* show that a bias exists, but that it exists rather wanly. The *plurality* of stories are about "Church Happenings" — nuts and bolts stories that carry little positive or negative spin. The principal focus of the news is the papacy, not a story topic one usually associates with "bad press" for the Church. And the "Church hierarchy" is cited more than 50 times as often as identified "Church dissidents"! (Computed from Table 6.) An amazing statistic really.

On balance, the news agenda and the news spin do go against the Church, but in what is a reasonably close call. According to the tables, the split in opinions expressed by the news sources in stories about sexual morality, birth control, and abortion run about 45-55 "against" the Church. That is something akin to a tie in news reporting, and while there does seem to be a shift away from the Church — press coverage becomes somewhat more negative with the passing of time — it is not a very pronounced or even continuous shift toward the negative.

Actually, Lichter, Amundson and Lichter have it just about right, given their own data. "[O]pinions in the media were tilted against the Church's teachings." But "[t]he news was certainly not all bad for the Church. . . . Members of the hierarchy were cited; official teachings were. . . presented; and on some issues . . . the Church's teaching was endorsed by a majority of sources." Nowhere is there any comparison to the Nazis.

As a matter of news content per se, I would say that there is (was) bias against the Church in the major news media. But at these levels of bias, it ought to be more an irritation to the Church than any serious liability.

Second, there is an inherent problem with any content analytic research, one that is especially acute in our instance. That problem involves the *scope* of the study.

By definition, content analysis looks only at that which it looks upon. But the news is only part of a newspaper; more important, the news is only a fraction of the mass medium content we call television programming. And news is practically nothing as a fraction of movies or film.

Forget for a moment that CMPA was limited in the number of years it could include in its analysis or the number of sources it could analyze. Let us consider a much larger problem than how many newspapers, how many news programs, etc.

CMPA demonstrates that Father Charles Curran, a leading clerical dissident of the 1970s and 1980s was cited no fewer than 30 times within the scope of their analysis. That *is* interesting. And the numbers become even more intriguing when one discovers that Father Andrew Greeley, the consummate "bad boy" of the American priesthood these last dozen years, was cited 21 times.

But — and this is crucial — what about the other parts of the mass media? How big were these dissenters in their programming? I am not sure from the data how many times CBS Evening News mentioned Curran or Greeley or for that matter Archbishop Raymond Hunthausen. But I am pretty certain that *if* one excludes ABC's Father Dowling and the Father Dowling mystery series from the content of television, one is going to make a big mistake when deciding what television is doing to public attitudes toward the Church or priests or Catholics. Father Dowling gets at least as much "time" as Curran, Greeley, and Hunthausen combined.

A few years back, one clever pollster asked the American public about some of our leading jurists. The poll indicated that somewhere between two and three times as many Americans could identify Judge Wapner of the "People's Court" as could identify William Rehnquist of the real Supreme Court.

Actually, many of my liberal friends took great comfort in that finding, Wapner being more to their philosophical tastes. But what that finding about public knowledge of jurists implies is that *any* conclusion one draws about TV news' impact on public attitudes toward the Church has got to look not just at Father Curran's press coverage but also at Father Dowling's mysteries! Does anybody here believe that, among the non-Catholic population in the United States, Father Curran is as widely recognized as Father Dowling? And we have not even begun to factor in the bonus that accrues to the Church for the replays we see of *The Bells of St. Mary's* or *Going My Way* or *White Christmas*, or the entire slew of movies with Bing Crosby as the saintly priest.

But Bing Crosby notwithstanding I would like to put my final emphasis on the third factor: the real reason that drives me to believe that news content about the Church probably does not matter much.

At the risk of engaging in tautology, let me state my case almost as definition. The bias does not matter much because it does not seem to matter much. In short, I find no persuasive evidence that news coverage is causing any increase in anti-Catholic sentiment or any decrease in Catholic social or political viability in the American system.

For the last half dozen years I have helped the Times Mirror Company, owners of the *Los Angeles Times*, and *Newsday*, among others, do national surveys about politics and social values. In 1990 we did one of our largest studies ever, interviewing over 3,000 people in face-to-face interviews, with each interview lasting well over an hour. In that survey, as in many of our surveys, religion and religious values were major concerns. And, as a consequence, questions about Catholics and Catholicism were very much in abundance in the 1990 survey.

And how did Catholics and Catholicism do in our 1990 survey of "The People, Press and Politics"? Saints be praised! Catholics and Catholicism came out pretty much on top.

Take a look at Figure 1 (p. 182). The Church ranks number one in terms of favorability when compared with ten other national groups or institutions! Especially interesting, I think, is the comparison between "the Church" (89 percent favorable) and Evangelical Christians (53 percent favorable).

But look again, this time at Figure 2 (p. 183), and see who is the most-favored person in our 1990 survey. Yes, His Holiness, John Paul II. Only Vaclav Havel comes within ten points of the Pope. Only one person in the history of our polling has done better than John Paul II — General Schwarzkopf. And Schwarzkopf has yet to prove his "staying power" the way the Pope has done for at least a decade.

Finally, look at Figures 3 (p. 184) and 4 (p. 185). These data show how well Catholics are doing in real world electoral politics, a special concern to me, a government professor living here in Washington. The trend is clear. Over time, and beginning at just the point when CMPA begins its analysis, Catholics consistently do better at getting elected to the House and to the Senate.

Given the size of the American Catholic population and the very sectarian nature of American Protestantism, it is true, of course, that Catholics are *always* (in modern times) the largest religious denomination in Congress. But these numbers show that whatever the news media may have been saying about Catholics and their Church since the early 1960s, it has not mattered very much. More than a quarter (27 percent) of the 102nd Congress is Catholic. In 1963, that figure was but 18 percent, a third less!

If the test of a pudding is in the eating, the test of an image is in the polling. If the negative spin and bias in the news media mattered much, we would have to predict that the polls and the electoral returns would be running against the Church and its people. But there is no such trend.

Perhaps one might want to say that the bad press does not hurt the Church's image, per se, or even its electability, but that bad press hurts Church attendance or diminishes the number of men and women who might seek a religious life if the image of the Church were not so much under attack. But does it make any sense to say that "bad press" and "news bias" against the Church affect Catholics, but that they affect nobody else? Doubtful.

My guess remains that the Church does well in public regard, and Catholics do well in American politics, for reasons that have little to do with the press per se. And even if the issue is "the media," then I say, again and finally, that the bias is fairly paltry and the entertainment media more than make up for the negative spin that appears on CBS Evening News or in *Time* or even at *The Washington Post*; make that *especially* at *The Washington Post*.

Nobody likes bad press. And every group probably ought to pay somebody to find out in precise terms how their press is going. But in the end what matters, at least in the secular life, is what people think. As of today, what Americans think of the Pope, the Church and the Catholic community is not what one would predict from reading the newspapers or watching network news.

Now, the last thing I want to say is this — and I had no intention of saying it until Brent Bozell spoke. He gave a stirring speech at the end about what you should do: Get up out of your seats and say you're mad as hell and you're not going to take it anymore.

I am not here as your political consultant, and I am not suggesting that you stop checks that might have been sent to Brent Bozell for his political advice. But I would suggest that you might get a new political advisor. If Brent Bozell is giving advice to you, I strongly urge you to find political consultation in other quarters. For if I go to my political advisor and say, "My Pope has a 90 percent favorability score, and my Church has an 88 percent favorability score — what do you recommend?"; and he says, "I recommend warfare against the mass media" — then I suggest that he has misunderstood the public's regard for your leadership and your institution. He also has not understood what is to my mind a basic fact, namely, war with the media usually does not help. If nine out of ten Americans think Pope John Paul II is doing a good job, the last thing you want to do is go half-cocked, criticizing the American media for the way they have covered the Pope or the Church or the hierarchy. It could get a lot worse than it shows here.

Figure 1
Favorability Scores (% Favorable) for Major Political Institutions (May 1990)

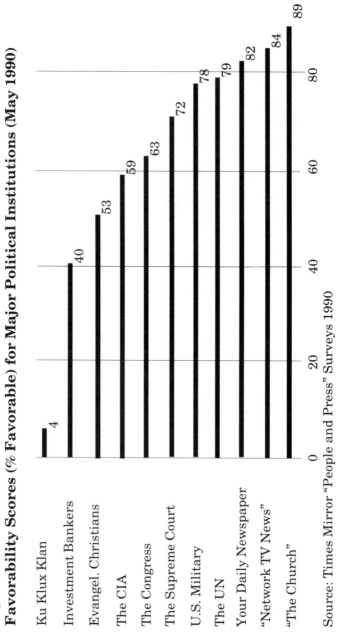

Ku Klux Klan	4
Investment Bankers	40
Evangel. Christians	53
The CIA	59
The Congress	63
The Supreme Court	72
U.S. Military	78
The UN	79
Your Daily Newspaper	82
"Network TV News"	84
"The Church"	89

Source: Times Mirror "People and Press" Surveys 1990

Figure 2
Favorability Scores (% Favorable) for Famous Leaders (May 1990)

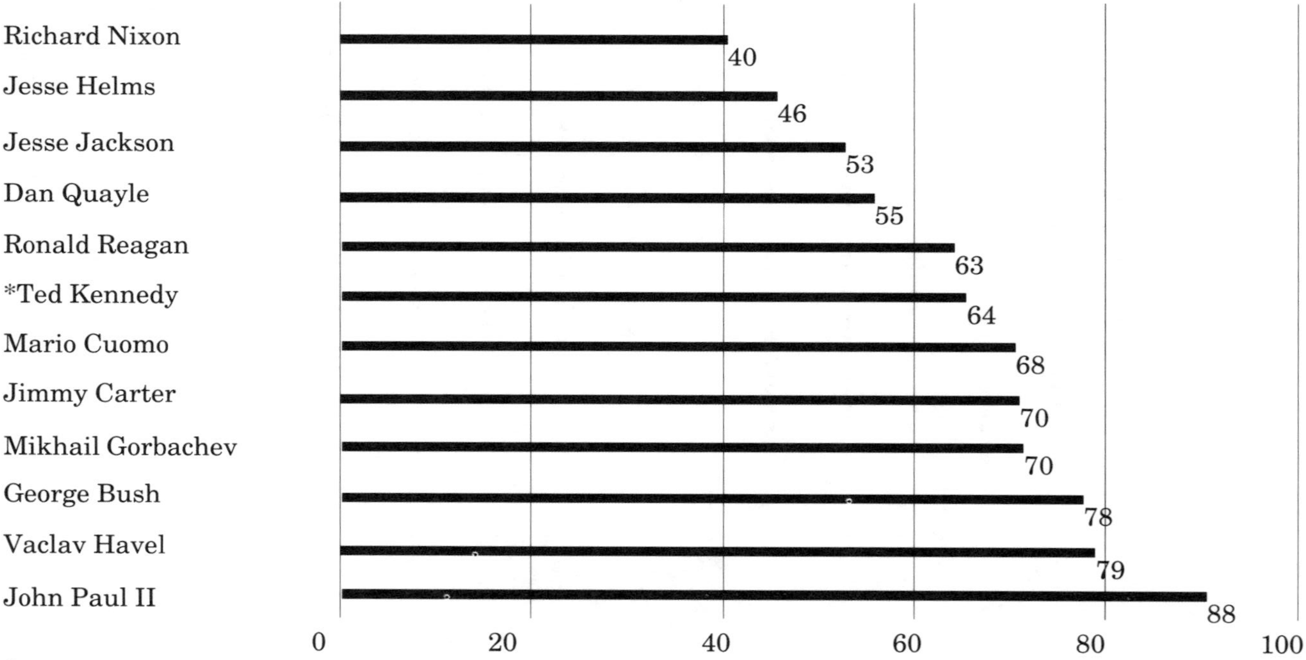

Leader	Score
Richard Nixon	40
Jesse Helms	46
Jesse Jackson	53
Dan Quayle	55
Ronald Reagan	63
*Ted Kennedy	64
Mario Cuomo	68
Jimmy Carter	70
Mikhail Gorbachev	70
George Bush	78
Vaclav Havel	79
John Paul II	88

Source: Times Mirror "People and Press" Surveys 1990 *Kennedy figure obtained months before Palm Beach episode

Figure 3
Number of Catholic Members of the House 1963-1991

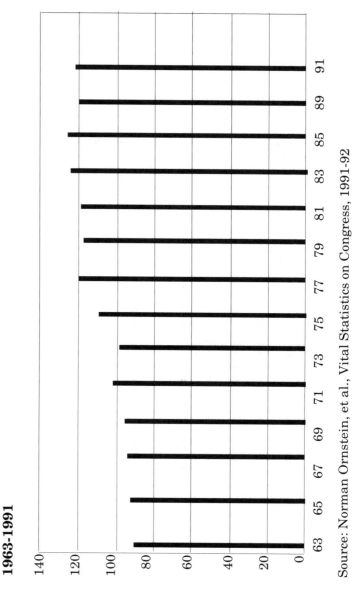

Source: Norman Ornstein, et al., Vital Statistics on Congress, 1991-92

The Conference

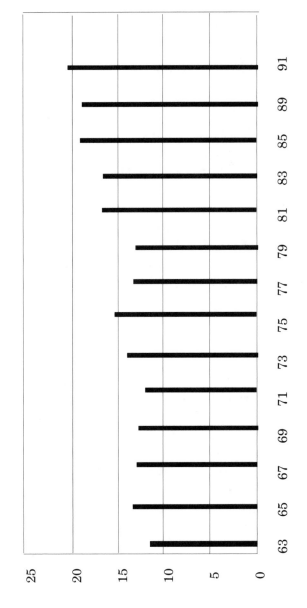

Figure 4
Number of Catholic Members of the Senate
1963-1991

Source: Norman Ornstein, et al., Vital Statistics on Congress, 1991-92

Response to Michael J. Robinson

The Honorable K. D. Whitehead

KENNETH D. WHITEHEAD, an author and translator, is a former career Foreign Service Officer, and has served as Deputy Director of the Smithsonian Institution, Executive Vice President of Catholics United for the Faith, and Assistant Secretary for Postsecondary Education, U.S. Department of Education.

I AM GLAD Professor Robinson liked *Media Coverage of the Catholic Church*. I too thought the study was an excellent one, and, for a non-specialist such as myself, also an enlightening one. I am therefore pleased to have this judgment confirmed, at least in general terms, by a "practicing content analyst," as Professor Robinson describes himself, who has found the study to be "scholarly, objective, and valid."

I earnestly hope that I do not like the study merely because it tends to confirm in so many respects what has often distressed me, as a Catholic, during a good part of my adult life, namely, the fact of the "bad press" which the Church seems fated to get. What was once merely a subjective impression for me has now been shown with some qualifications to be a pretty well established fact.

There is also the question of degree, of course. As Professor Robinson points out, "the data in this study show that the bias against the Church is not all that bad." Although I do not entirely agree with this — more on that as we go along — I do concede that Professor Robinson has a point. But I see even that point somewhat differently.

One of the conclusions I brought away from the study, whether or not it was ever in the intentions of the authors, was the conviction that the Church's acknowledged bad press may well result from something beyond mere bias; it may be at least partly rooted in some of the fundamental assumptions and practices of the modern mass media; bias as such may not be the only or even the principal reason why the Catholic Church keeps coming out "on the losing side of the issue debate reported in the media."

One of the difficulties arises out of the nature of the Church herself. The Church claims to teach with authority a universal message of salvation. Quite obviously, how one sees the Church is going to differ considerably depending upon how one views that claim. The very notion of an ultimate, saving truth for mankind revealed "once for all" (Jude 3) and handed down within a living entity, the Church, is simply alien to what seems to be one of the fundamental assumptions of the modern media. For the media often seem to take it for granted that all truth must necessarily emerge out of the modern marketplace of ideas, while rarely granting that the corner some of these same media often have on that same marketplace of ideas sometimes means in practice that some perhaps worthy ideas never get a chance to emerge into the light of day at all.

As the study before us documents, the media automatically look to multiple "sources" as a matter of course for the information that is to be reported — too often, as if all such sources were somehow equivalent; as if, in the context of our present discussion, the views of a Father Charles Curran might possibly weigh equally in the balance with the teachings of a Paul VI in a papal encyclical. While there can be no objection whatsoever to reporting the dissenting views of a Father Curran because he has in fact dissented, part of the real and full truth about reporting on the Catholic Church would also have to include the information that, in Catholic terms, the Pope is right on this particular issue and Father Curran is wrong.

In this connection, the fact that the official views of the leaders of the Church do get amply reported, a fact which both *Media Coverage of the Catholic Church* and Professor Robinson make much of, is not really terribly helpful in a context in which these same leaders are depicted as "conservative, oppressive, and out of touch." The views of the Ayatollah Khomeini, for example, or those of successive governments of South Africa, have always similarly been abundantly reported, but hardly in a manner calculated to elicit any sympathy.

Again, the modern media tend to represent modern democracy and representative institutions as an assumed norm with which the Church somehow always has to be compared. It is never quite clear why the reputation of the Church has to suffer because of the lack of "democratic" or "representative" features, since the modern corporation, the modern military, the modern university, to name a few examples, to say nothing of the media empires studied by the Center for Media and Public Affairs — *Time, The New York Times, The Washington Post*, and CBS — are themselves in no way democratic nor are they expected by anybody to be democratic.

Similarly, the media tendency, again documented in the study before us, to report on the life and activities of an entity such as the Catholic Church in typically "political" terms — as if conflicts and questions of who gets what, how, when, and where were the main features of an institution primarily and professedly engaged in the business of the sanctification and salvation of its own communicants — is yet another distortion of reality. It arises out of the way too many media people insist on viewing an institution which may resemble a political entity, and which undeniably has its own kind of internal politics as well, as necessarily impinging on politics and society as a whole; but which is fundamentally a very different kind of organization than it is too often assumed to be. Any reporter who approached the 1985 Extraordinary Synod of Bishops imagining that the main point about it was a Ratzinger "crackdown" or an attempt to "roll back Vatican II" was not only going to be disappointed; he was also going to be quite incapable of reporting the real truth about the Synod to the public at large. This not so much a matter of bias as of ignorance, I believe.

I could go on in this vein. A careful reading of *Media Coverage of the Catholic Church* opened up, for me at least, a number of such lines of thought which seem as important for the modern media and their claim to serve truth as for the Church and her ability to operate in our society. But since I have been asked here primarily to provide a "response" to Professor Robinson's paper — itself a very original, interesting, and enlightening contribution to our common subject — I shall comment briefly in the time remaining on each one of the three points which Professor Robinson has addressed to the three authors of the study.

1) "The bias against the Church is not all that bad." Even if media bias, as documented by the study, does not add up to an image of Catholics "only slightly better than that of Nazis," the study does pretty thoroughly

demonstrate that the all-too-typical presentation of the Church is one of an institution that is reactionary, authoritarian, and irrelevant.

Is this supposed to be somehow comforting to Catholics, or even acceptable to us as Americans: that while we may not be quite as bad as Nazis, the accepted public image of the Church we belong to — one of the oldest continuously existing institutions in the world — is to be that of an institution that is hidebound, authoritarian, and no longer of any possible interest to anyone who is truly up-to-date about things (although, in addition to being one of the oldest, it is also one of the most extended and far-flung of all human institutions as well)? If the degree of bias exhibited here is truly "not all that bad," in Professor Robinson's words, let us be thankful that it is at least not any worse!

For my part, I would ask what other community or institution in America is routinely presented in the media in such a taken-for-granted unfavorable light? Our fundamentalist Christian brethren, for instance? Racists? However that may be, the theory and practice of "media fairness" in America might at the very least undergo a re-examination here. (Part of the problem for some of us non-media people is the number of media people we encounter who quite sincerely do not seem to understand that there is anything wrong or unfair about the way they approach certain topics such as the Catholic Church or the pro-life movement.)

2) "The 'news' is only part of a newspaper . . . [and] a fraction of the mass medium content we call television programming." I basically agree with the point Professor Robinson makes here: that entertainment can and does often present a very different image of the Church, and moreover, many more hours on television are devoted to

this kind of programming. There can be little doubt that the Father Dowling mysteries can offset the impression created by a report on the plight of Archbishop Hunthausen on the evening news.

However, it is also true that entertainment can also reinforce the negative image of the Church. While Catholics cannot be anything but wholly pleased by the depiction of Thomas More in *A Man for All Seasons* or of the labor priest in *On the Waterfront*, say, other films, such as *The Godfather* or *Prizzi's Honor*, can equally convey the strong impression that some Catholics are accustomed to move directly from attending Mass to rubbing out their opponents in particularly bloody and gruesome ways.

I believe another study on the scale of *Media Coverage of the Catholic Church* itself would probably be necessary in order to provide us with solid, empirical knowledge of the degree to which entertainment media provide a positive or negative image of the Church. Meanwhile I do not believe that we can necessarily assume that the negative image verifiably conveyed in the news media is in fact offset by the entertainment media.

3) "The bias doesn't matter much. . ." I was both somewhat surprised as well as fascinated by the "favorability" tables included by Professor Robinson. I am gratified to learn that both Pope John Paul II and the Catholic Church rank so high in the public estimation, as measured by the *Los Angeles Times* surveys on politics and social values. As a result of these surveys, Professor Robinson finds "no persuasive evidence that news coverage is causing any increase in anti-Catholic sentiment."

Maybe. But this situation can also be viewed in another light. What is the evidence that the media are serving the truth in reporting about Catholics and the Church? Do the current "favorability" ratings of the present Pope and the

Church today arise out of the way these issues are presented in the media — or *in spite of* the way they are presented in the media? I do not believe it is either irrelevant or unfair to pose these questions. Pope John Paul II, for example, like Ronald Reagan, happens to be one of those public figures with a gift for speaking directly to people over the heads of media which, sometimes, appear to be trying to present him in a light rather more unfavorable than the one in which, in fact, the public ends up perceiving him. The same kind of thing was surely at work in the case of the very positive media image of Pope John XXIII — with perhaps the added factor that the media actually tended to be biased *in favor of* "good Pope John." I suspect very different results would be obtained if we examined the cases of Pope Paul VI or, especially, that of Pope Pius XII. Before drawing too definite a conclusion from the relationship between the favorability rating and the typical depiction in the media of the present pontiff, we would probably need to have comparable favorability ratings on Paul VI and Pius XII.

Finally, Professor Robinson makes his no doubt valid point about the increasing electability of Catholics to Congress as indicating the lack of any pronounced public bias against Catholics as such. From the Church's point of view, though, getting her members elected to Congress or to other leadership positions is hardly one of her primary goals or preoccupations as a religious institution. We may scrutinize from one end to the other the very considerable body of teachings produced by the official Church at all levels, and nowhere will we find much, or even any, attention given to such goals or pursuits as getting Catholics elected to Congress. Whether some observers ever wish to credit it or not, the Church does see herself as being engaged primarily in the soul-saving business, while also trying to do or encourage whatever good she or her members can accomplish in this world in the meantime.

In any case, pertinent to our present subject, the Church's image is scarcely enhanced when, as too frequently happens today, some of the Catholics who do get elected to office today end up taking public positions which are anything but "Catholic" on controversial subjects such as abortion. This phenomenon has been a major media issue, of course: We need think only of the running controversy between New York Cardinal John O'Connor and vice presidential candidate Geraldine Ferraro. Indeed, it is ironic that Virginia's Governor L. Douglas Wilder should have come out with his view that Catholics can perhaps not really be trusted in public office in this country owing to their "allegiance" to the Pope — this at a time when some Catholic politicians are finding it necessary to declare, in effect, that they don't necessarily have any allegiance to the Pope.

There is an important question of truth in reporting here. The media are usually quick to expose, say, prominent televangelists when it turns out that they have not been practicing what they preach. However, when Catholic politicians agree with the U.S. Supreme Court that what Vatican Council II taught was "an abominable crime" (*Gaudium et Spes*, 51) is somehow, suddenly, courtesy of Mr. Justice Blackmun, "a woman's right to choose," there is hardly ever any suggestion that these Catholic politicians are being dishonest about the degree to which they actually do profess the faith they claim to profess. Rather, these Catholic politicians are often celebrated as conscientious martyrs to tyrannical and retrograde Church authority.

I am not raising this question here in order to castigate these politicians for conduct of which I disapprove —

although I *do* disapprove of it — but merely to make a point pertinent to our present discussion. The media tend to present these Catholic politicians in ways which allow them to take maximum advantage of their religious and ethnic affiliations, while not being required to bear the burden of Catholic Church teachings perceived to be unpopular with the public at large.

I believe this is a serious media question, and I could cite others. The existence of such questions leads, I believe, to a conclusion contrary to the one I take to be Professor Robinson's final point. The media *do* matter for an institution such as the Catholic Church, as she attempts to live her special kind of life and carry on with her own announced mission on these shores, under a First Amendment which is supposed to guarantee her a constitutional right to do so. In this perspective, the media matter a great deal, and therefore what Professor Robinson calls the "fine study," *Media Coverage of the Catholic Church*, also matters.

Indeed, it seems to me that the media's own claim to serve the truth is at stake in the way an institution such as the Catholic Church is treated by and in the media, quite apart from the whole question of how much it all matters to the Church herself.

Experiencing the Media Culture

Mary Ellen Bork

MARY ELLEN BORK, a free-lance writer and lecturer specializing in issues affecting Catholic life, is the wife of Judge Robert H. Bork. She is a Director of the Catholic Campaign for America and of the Notre Dame Catechetical Institute, Arlington, Va., and Councilor of the Catholic League's Washington Chapter.

PERHAPS IT WOULD be well to begin with a small confession. If you have had the opportunity to experience the media personally — either in a happy encounter or a not so happy one — your views are forever colored by that experience. It is just possible that mine have been.

Never did I imagine, for example, that journalists and TV cameramen would camp in the street in front of our house from six in the morning to eight at night, shouting questions at us whenever we emerged. Just bringing in the morning newspapers became a test of fortitude. Nor did I anticipate that after the Senate vote an ABC camera crew would follow our car into the garage, and I would be unable to resist the urge to defend my husband for the nightly news. Or that I would fend off nightly phone calls from Barbara Walters, one of them at midnight, seeking an interview after the White House had encouraged her.

One of the things I remember best is that in the last week two motorcycles and one automobile — representing the three major networks — followed us wherever we went, to the courthouse or to a restaurant. The motorcyclists wore helmets and goggles, and they looked quite ominous as they tailed us without pause.

You might say that the experience was negative, but no more so than reading the papers in the morning to see what *The New York Times* and *The Washington Post* were saying. The press, we quickly saw, was on the hunt. Early on, I was under instructions simply to hand Bob the sports sections and nothing else. I, on the other hand, read the columnists on the opinion pages for the news, and the front pages for the editorials.

The effect, I must say, was to make me take the media less seriously than I once did. Harry Truman learned that lesson. He said his heart went out to all those serious and well-meaning people who read the papers assiduously and were under the impression that they knew what was happening in their time.

Sometimes I even feel as Chesterton did when he remarked that ". . .we all know that thousands of good men accept these ethics of the journalist, just as thousands of others accept the equally disputed ethics of the barrister. To my mind both are dubious, but those of the barrister much the more defensible, because he puts on a fantastic costume and stands in a particular place, by way of warning the public that for a certain definite period he is not going to tell the truth. If all the insincere opinions in the press were invariably printed in red ink, we should have something like the same fair warning."[1] But that is not the way things work.

The media culture we live in is a truly modern

phenomenon. The combination of instant availability of images from almost any part of the world and our insatiable hunger for news on every conceivable topic creates a culture dominated by visual images, sound bites and packaged events. This media culture cultivates the illusion that we are well-informed if we read the newspapers and watch enough TV, listen to talk shows and know headlines.

We have become accustomed to a culture dominated by what Daniel Boorstin, former Librarian of Congress, calls "pseudo-events," pre-packaged, pre-arranged press conferences, news conferences, and planned events that make up much of what we call "news." We do not gather news any more, we make it. We have the means to make news twenty-four hours a day. Boorstin contends that our eagerness for news somehow satisfies our unreal demand upon the world for "more than the world can give us." We are willing to live with illusions which give us a sense of power.[2]

Be that as it may, our expectations about news are palpable. "Every American knows the anticipation with which he picks up his morning newspaper at breakfast or opens his evening paper before dinner, or listens to the newscasts every hour on the hour as he drives across country, or watches his favorite commentator on television interpret the events of the day."[3] Responding to this expectation is an army of newsmen and journalists, the exigencies of whose lives are probably not well understood by most people. Some writers have observations on their vocation.

This reminds me of Evelyn Waugh's character William Boot in his novel *Scoop*. Boot is a nature writer become war correspondent. He is rushed to the war zone in Ishmaelia in East Africa. The London-based newspaper, *The Beast*, has hired him to cover the action. The owner of the paper, Lord Copper, explains to William the policy of the paper: "I never hamper my correspondents in any way. What the British public wants first, last, and all the time is News. Remember that the Patriots are in the right and are going to win. *The Beast* stands by them four square. But they must win quickly. The British public has no interest in a war which drags on indecisively. A few sharp victories, some conspicuous acts of personal bravery on the Patriot side and a colorful entry into the capital. That is *The Beast* policy for the war."[4]

Knowing little about journalism, Boot relies on his colleague, Corker, a wire-service writer, who explains to him:

> "I envy you — working for a paper. You only have to worry about getting your story in time for the first edition. We have to race each other all day."
>
> "But the papers can't use your reports any earlier than ours."
>
> "'No, but they use the one that comes in first."
>
> "But if it's exactly the same as the one that came in second and third and fourth and they are all in time for the same edition. . .?"
>
> Corker looked at him sadly. "You know, you've got a lot to learn about journalism. Look at it this way. News is what a chap who doesn't care much about anything wants to read. And it's only news until he's read it. After that it's dead. We're paid to supply news. If someone else has sent a story before us, our story isn't news. Of course there's color. Color is just a lot of bull's-eyes about nothing. It's easy to write and easy to read but it costs too much in cabling so we have to go slow on that. See? "[5]

No war was actually happening, and Boot's editor and publisher importuned him daily for news, especially of victories. A German girl convinced him to pay her to find some news, since she knew the governess to the President's children and a Minister's hairdresser. She discovers that the President has been locked in his bedroom by Dr. Benito, director of the Press Bureau, and an enigmatic Russian, until he signs some important papers. The President's habit was to let work pile up and stay in his room for a couple of days to complete it. His two friends put out the word that he has not appeared because he is drunk. She also found that a couple of people were suffering from the plague. Boot decided to make news out of this for *The Beast*.

> He sat at the table, stood up, sat down again, stared gloomily at the wall for some minutes, lit his pipe, and then, laboriously, with a single first finger and his heart heavy with misgiving, he typed the first news story of his meteoric career. No one observing that sluggish and hesitant composition could have guessed that this was a moment of history — of legend, to be handed down among the great traditions of his trade, told and retold over the milk-bars of Fleet Street, quoted in books of reminiscence, held up as a model to aspiring pupils of Correspondence Schools of Profitable Writing, perennially fresh in the jaded memories of a hundred editors; the moment when Boot began to make good.
>
> PRESS COLLECT BEAST LONDON he wrote. NOTHING MUCH HAS HAPPENED EXCEPT TO THE PRESIDENT WHO HAS BEEN IMPRISONED IN HIS OWN PALACE BY REVOLUTIONARY JUNTA HEADED BY SUPERIOR BLACK CALLED BENITO AND RUSSIAN JEW WHO BANNISTER SAYS IS UP TO NO GOOD THEY SAY HE IS DRUNK WHEN HIS CHILDREN TRY TO SEE HIM BUT GOVERNESS SAYS MOST UNUSUAL LOVELY SPRING WEATHER BUBONIC PLAGUE RAGING.[6]

His coverage of the war in Ishmaelia was lauded in London and he soon returned to England where he was knighted.

Samuel Clemens was also an observer of the press. As an old man traveling in England, he had to deal with the press about a rumor that he was dying. American editors cabled their London representatives to rush to Clemens's apartment and send back the full sensational story.

> There was nothing the matter with me and each in his turn was astonished, and not gratified, to find me reading and smoking in my

study and worth next to nothing as a text for transatlantic news. One of these men was a gentle and kindly and grave and sympathetic Irishman, who hid his disappointment the best he could and tried to look glad and told me that his paper, the *Evening Sun*, had cabled him that it was reported in New York that I was dead. What should he cable in reply? I said, "Say the report is exaggerated."

He never smiled, but went solemnly away and sent the cable in those exact words. The remark hit the world pleasantly.[7]

It is further reported that "Twain was curious as to the wording of the cablegrams which the reporters arrived clutching. He managed to read the cable held by the *New York World's* man, which read 'If Mark Twain dying send five hundred words. If dead send a thousand.' "[8]

The Washington news scene has many interesting characters, among them the press secretary. In *White House Mess* Christopher Buckley describes President Thomas Tucker's press secretary, Mike Feely:

> He had been with the President the longest, having joined the campaign well ahead of all the johnny-come-latelies. Feels, as we called him, had come up through the hawsepipe, and had served briefly — four days — as Geraldine Ferraro's press secretary. (He had the most unpleasant memories of that experience, apparently.) He was a pugnacious fellow of Irish descent, with a florid complexion and unruly hair. (I often had to ask him to brush it before a press conference.) Feels was not a man of delicate sensibilities. I suppose press secretaries can't afford them. His trademark was his propensity to resign. His cries of 'This is an outrage!' were a familiar sound of the Spirit of Greatness, our converted Boeing 707. One day he resigned twice. His foibles amused the Governor, and he was very good with the collection of jackals and unscrupulous swine that make up the White House press corps; ladies excluded, of course."[9]

At the outset, I told you about those ominous, helmeted and goggled motorcyclists who trailed us for days on behalf of the TV networks. They turned out not to be as ominous as they looked. They followed us to the White House where everybody expected my husband to announce the withdrawal of his nomination. Instead, he announced that he was staying in to take the vote, even knowing certainly that he would lose. On the way back from the White House, we looked back at our pursuers, and one gave us an enthusiastic thumbs-up signal with a gloved hand. We were enormously cheered. The minions of the press, or some of them, had hearts, too.

These writers — Chesterton, Boorstin, Waugh, Clemens, and Buckley, among others — give us an insight into our media culture. If I have stressed some of the more negative insights, that is because it is more fun. But no one doubts the great value of a free press in a democratic society. My husband once wrote an opinion in which he said: "The American press is extraordinarily free and vigorous, as it should be. It should be, not because it is free of inaccuracy, oversimplification, and bias, but because the alternative to that freedom is worse than those failings."[10]

Our media may get a lot of things wrong, but they also get a lot of things right. And they are a necessary, though not a sufficient, protection from government that may become too domineering. Thomas Jefferson said that if the choice were between having government or having a free press, he would choose the press. Fortunately, we face no such choice. Jefferson was sometimes given to extravagant rhetoric, but we see his point.

Endnotes

1. Marlin, George, ed., *More Quotable Chesterton* (San Francisco, 1988), p. 160.
2. Daniel Boorstin, *The Image* (New York, 1962), p. 9.
3. *Ibid.*
4. Evelyn Waugh, *Scoop* (London, 1964), p. 53.

5. *Ibid*, p. 79.
6. *Ibid*, p. 168.
7. Frank Muir, ed., *Oxford Book of Humorous Prose* (Oxford, 1990), p. 273.
8. *Ibid*, p. 273.
9. Christopher Buckley, *White House Mess* (New York, 1986), p. 15.
10. *Ollman* v. *Evans*.

The Conference

The Discussion

---

*Following is an edited transcript of the discussion. Be-
cause of the format of the conference and the schedules of
particular speakers, not all of the papers and responses
were followed immediately by dialogue among the conference participants. All, however, were subject to discussion, which took place during both the morning and the
afternoon sessions.*

Michael McManus: I have some criticisms of the study,
which I want to go into in a minute, but first I have to
explain who I am because I have a kind of unique
perspective on this issue. I write a nationally syndicated
column called *Ethics and Religion*, which is now in about
125 newspapers, and I market the column myself as well as
write it.

The criticism I have of the report is that it draws its
generalizations and conclusions on the basis of only looking
at *The Washington Post* and *The New York Times* and CBS
and *Time* magazine. Certainly those are giant media in our
world, but thank God they aren't the only media.

We have 1,600 daily newspapers in this country, and I
think that the report, in trying to make these
generalizations about the bias of the media, really looked at
too limited a sample of newspapers for example.

I also say that — and this is a private comment, for
myself — I looked over about fifty or so of the columns I've

written on the Catholic Church, and they were more positive than negative. For example, on the dispute with Father [Charles] Curran, it seemed to me the Church was within its rights to say, "Hey, he's at the Catholic University! We don't think you're teaching Catholic truth, get out!" I praised the bishops' reports on war and peace, on the economy, which is really a study about poverty.

On the issue of pornography, where *The Washington Post* didn't even cover the last week of the Attorney General's commission on pornography here, I covered it every day in Washington when they were making their conclusions. *The Washington Post* wasn't there for five days. Neither was *The New York Times*. *Time* magazine showed up for half a day. But there were some of us who were trying to cover the story with some seriousness, and report that pornography does in fact have harmful consequences. This is a point of view that I think the Church shares.

I have been critical in columns on celibacy and other matters which seemed to me harmful to the Church itself. But it's a gross exaggeration to say that all the media is hostile to the Catholic point of view, because at least this reporter has been able to get a different point of view into papers with about five million circulation.

I think that Mr. Harwood, in commenting that the press reflects the society, is wrong in the extreme. We are a culture, according to Gallup, in which 69 percent of the people are members of a church or a synagogue. Seventy-eight percent believe that religion is important. Ninety percent pray. Forty-three percent of the whole country, 110 million people, attended services in the last ten days, according to George Gallup.

You would never know that by reading *The Washington Post*. You would never know that by reading any of the secular media that this report rightly criticizes as being biased. There's not one single network that has a single full-time person covering this world of morality and faith, which is so important to American people.

By contrast, according to *U.S. News and World Report*, only four percent of Americans go to a sports event in a week. And just look at the space devoted to sports in the newspaper.

This subject [religion] is enormously interesting, and yet it is almost dismissed. I can't even find the page which *The Washington Post* provides on Saturday — it doesn't even tell you in its index where it is. You have to look. It is E7 or something. You can hardly find the darn thing.

And then when it covers it, it never covers it as if faith makes a difference in life. There is an alternative point of view which is never reflected in these media. For example, last week the Board of Education of New York City voted not only to give out condoms to every one of the 260,000 high school students but to bar the parents from blocking their own kids' access to those condoms. The idea is that condoms reduce teen pregnancy.

But this is poor reporting. The fact of the matter is, according to Planned Parenthood's own magazine, *Family Planning Perspectives*, a recent study of five or six cities which have given away condoms, such as Gary and Dallas and San Francisco, found no impact on teen pregnancy. On the other hand, there is a series of courses which make a case for abstinence and which actually work. For example, Sex Respect, a course used in more than a thousand public high schools, increases the percentage of kids who say they want to be sexually abstinent from about 20 to 40 percent. More important, a year afterward the kids who have taken the course are only half as likely to be sexually active as those who have not.

What has been lacking is a seriousness of trying to report these subjects by the national news media that this report rightly indicts. There are those of us who are trying to present the other side of it — only we're running into a stone wall in trying to get our stuff published in certain publications.

Reed Irvine: Mr. Harwood, you justified the preponderance of quotes on the issue of birth control on the grounds that this reflects public opinion. Is it your view that the quotes that we find in the media in general reflect public opinion on all issues, or do they more nearly reflect the opinions of the reporters who seek out the people that they're quoting?

For example, have you observed that the preponderance of quotes on issues like capital punishment reflect the overwhelming views of the public that capital punishment is right? Or, would you say the quotes on gun control reflect the views of, as some polls indicate, a very strong support for the right to keep and bear arms? Do you think that reporters study the polls and then go out and say, "Well let's find quotes that tell us what 70 or 80 percent of the public think," and try to get 70 or 80 percent of the quotes reflecting public opinion?

Richard Harwood: Your question has to do with the universe and all that's in it, but if you will be a little specific: Do reporters read the opinion polls and then adjust the number of quotations they use accordingly? No.

Irvine: Well, you said that the deck was not stacked on the birth control issue because it was simply reflecting public opinion. Then what is a reporter supposed to do? Is he supposed to reflect public opinion, or is he supposed to give equal time to the differing points of view? How does he make up his mind as to what the proportion pro and con quotes is going to be?

Harwood: Someone else used a phrase about the function of journalism which I will borrow: It is to attempt to set the face of the age. If we were to present a report indicating that, let us say, the position of the Catholic Church on birth control was overwhelmingly supported by people of the world, and that people of an opposite view are heretics and a demented minority, that would not be setting the face of the age.

Irvine: There's been a major controversy over the showing over three PBS stations in this country of the film "Stop the Church." It's raging in Los Angeles where KCT showed it. It's raging in New York. I suspect you're familiar with the film. It is based on the gays' disruption of the Mass. . .

Harwood: I heard about that. Yes.

Irvine: And it's been very severely criticized as being a strong anti-Catholic film. Now you can say, I suppose, that because it's Los Angeles and it's New York, this would not be a matter that ought to be carried by the *Post*. But if there were an anti-Semitic film shown by the PBS station in New York or in Los Angeles, I wonder if that would not get reflected more in national reporting. It wouldn't be treated as purely a local issue, would it?

Harwood: Are you suggesting, like [Louis] Farrakhan, that there's some Jewish conspiracy at work here?

Irvine: No, I'm suggesting there's a much greater sensitivity to anti-Semitism than there is to anti-Catholicism. This is a very anti-Catholic film, and yet it's not given the same attention, I'm suggesting, as if it were an anti-Semitic film. I wonder if that doesn't reflect some kind of attitude that deserves attention. . . .

Robert Royal: I'm very grateful to Michael Robinson for this material, because I was not previously aware of it. It is quite striking, I think, for some of us who have a grimmer view of what coverage of the Catholic Church is like than the actuality is.

It may be forcing the point somewhat, but I couldn't help thinking, when you were talking about how popular the Pope is, of a story G.K. Chesterton once told about why the King of England is so popular. Everybody said, "He doesn't do anything, and after all we've got all these politicians who are energetic and intelligent and are doing things." Chesteron said, "You have to understand that the basic situation in England is this. There are people pushing and shoving and shouting at one another at Hyde Park Corner about what will be the next step in English society. And just as they're about to come to blows and have the whole thing erupt into a riot, a carriage goes by, and in that carriage there is sitting a very stately figure, and they all applaud. And the reason is that they know that is the one man in England who is not responsible for the condition in which they find themselves."

I think there has to be some of that in the popularity of the Pope. It's not surprising that Congress is unpopular with Americans. I think one of the reasons why those figures [on popularity] are so high for foreign figures in particular, like Gorbachev and Havel, is precisely that those people are not responsible for where we are.

But about the coverage. What lots of us who get upset about press coverage feel is that [the issue is] not so much a general, "Do you like the Pope or not? Is the Catholic Church okay or is it not okay?" There's much more of a kind of street-level struggle about: "Can I keep my kids from going off the deep end? Or can I make some serious arguments with my friends about the ways I think human life ought to be lived so that they do not, when they get pregnant, go off and kill the children in the womb?"

It's not only about the Catholic thing. One of the stories that brought home most graphically to me how biased certain media coverage is concerned a recent congress held by the Presbyterians in Baltimore. I have some colleagues at the Ethics and Public Policy Center who follow Protestant, Evangelical, Orthodox, and Jewish issues, as well as Catholic issues. I said to a friend of mine who follows the Presbyterians, "What kind of nuts are running the Presbyterian Church? I read these news stories that the Presbyterians are going to vote on totally accepting homosexuality, ordaining homosexuals, removing all stigma against it." And my colleague who follows the story closely said, "Yes, it's very worrisome." Then he went up to Baltimore, and in fact the vote was something like 485 of the delegates against this proposal and 15 or 20 — mostly on the committee that had prepared it — in favor.

I think that is the point at which most of these issues really get engaged. Lots of us feel the media create issues because they want certain points of view to succeed. When, in point of fact, if there were just more neutral reporting of where people actually stand, things would be a lot better and lots of us would be less exercised.

Michael Robinson: We discussed this last week in my American government class — 150 students, of whom about 100 are Catholic. Why is the Pope so popular? And, by the way, it ran about five to one, favorable to unfavorable.

One person said, "I think people like the Pope because he doesn't have any control over us. He leaves us alone." Well, the one in six who thought the Pope was not to be regarded favorably literally rose up out of their chairs and said, "This Pope, more than any other person around the world outside the United States, wants to influence my life. He wants to influence my reproductive decisions. He wants to influence my theological decisions. He wants to tell me who can and cannot perform Mass."

We discussed this at length. And in the end, while the one in six who were ideologically opposed to the Pope were not favorably predisposed, the five in six mostly felt the way I did: The guy's incredible. You shoot him, and he survives. On Christmas Day he gives his greetings to the world in 32 languages without note cards. He skis when he gets the chance to escape. He wrote folksongs and he still, I guess, writes some poetry.

The guy is charismatic, and I think that's part of the reason why we like the Pope. And the press has allowed us to know that he is charismatic, because he is charismatic and they like charisma.

Is this truth? Of course it's not truth. The press is not about truth. At best it's about fact. Years ago I gave up worrying about truth, and said, "If you give me some facts" — and they do — "that's good enough for me." And in a world of facts, the Pope does very well.

The second thing to say is that homosexuals do get a free ride from the press. There is no question in my mind that the press feels a certain sympathy for homosexuals. I'm not sure why. Maybe it's just part of the secularism that Lichter, I think, has identified as part of the underlying ideology.

But when the homosexuals in this country started to get AIDS, the press didn't ignore that story, and it was not a great story for homosexuals. And when the homosexuals tried to spin the press toward, "AIDS is just another example of why we have to be more sympathetic to homosexuals" — guess what? The facts came through, and the facts were that a homosexual life-style is associated with AIDS. That story has come through to the American people to the point where 42 percent of the public in our Times-Mirror survey in 1990 said they believe AIDS is

God's punishment for homosexual behavior.

What did the press do? First, it covered the homosexual movement, because it was big in the 1970s, and then it covered AIDS. Why? Because it was a real story. Did it cover it truthfully? I don't know. Did it cover it factually? More or less. What has been the result? American families don't want to send their children to school with little kids who have AIDS, whether they got it from homosexuality or not, and Americans are very afraid of homosexuals now in a way they weren't twenty years ago, because they may carry AIDS.

Now, a lot of this is nonsense hyped by the press. A lot of this has some patina of ideology. But I suggest to you that more fact and truth get through than you would believe.

Catholics have made a contribution to the United States, and Americans tend to rally to Catholics because of John Kennedy. They look at John Kennedy as a Catholic person who did good for his country. "Catholics are okay, and we'll even vote for one for President in the future."

Now, I go back to Jewish Cleveland and I hear, "This country is rampant with anti-Semitism." On the corner of Fourth and G where I live, blacks tell me this country is more anti-black and racist than it's ever been. And I say, "Go back to the nineteenth century. You want to know about anti-Catholicism? Look at the Know-Nothing Party, look at the Ku Klux Klan. You want to know about anti-Semitism? Go back and look at those two. You want to know about racism? Don't go to 1991; go to 1891, or 1791." And I will say this: The media have provided a purification that has helped us become a better, less racist, less ethnically hostile society.

Michael McManus: I want to make a couple of points

about your [Robinson's] generalizations.

The popularity of the Pope doesn't mean the Catholic Church is being treated well in the press. The popularity of the Pope, as you say, rests on his charisma and his courage, and his capacity to articulate. He does communicate through the media, and the media does cover him fairly well.

But the Church is not the Pope. The Church is 55 million people in the country, the kind of people that go to Mass. And what are they going there for? What are Protestants going to church for? They're going to draw closer to their God and to their fellow man. They're praying for their marriages. They're praying for their wayward children. They're praying for how to deal with a conflict with their boss.

And what we get from the media is not so much anti-Catholicism as anti-spiritual answers. "Punch him out!" "Abort the baby!" Euthanasia is now the newest rage. We're not told anywhere in the media how to live in a way that is loving. And attempts to try to present that point of view are in effect censored by a press and a television that is essentially anti-traditionalist. Its answer is faddish and quick.

And the stories — you cited Father Flanagan. That's 50 years ago. No one watches Father Flanagan any more. What we're watching now is "M.A.S.H.," in which the priest is ridiculed. What we watch now are stories of Protestant preachers who are sleeping with the lady behind the altar. There's hardly ever a positive depiction of people of faith in the entertainment media today.

Robinson: That simply isn't true. Father Dowling is the one priest on television.

McManus: But Father Dowling is hardly your average Catholic priest, and he's not depicting reality, in any sense, of what Catholics know to be a priest, or someone who comes from a spiritual point of view on any issue.

Robinson: Television is never going to do a story about a typical priest.

McManus: Why not?

Robinson: It's never going to do a story about a typical professor. It's never going to do a story about a typical businessperson. It's never going to do a story about anything typical. This is an entertainment medium that exists to show you something that is *not* typical.

Believe me, portrayals of American professors on television and in the movies are ludicrous, although they're not, for the most part, negative. Nor are the portrayals of men of the cloth in entertainment television negative.

Let me say this to you about "anti-traditional" and "anti-spiritual." You are correct. They are not traditional and they are not spiritual, and that is going to infuriate a person who is religious. And it's probably going to come across as a bias. It's infuriating, but in a way it is their job, because they're not in the business of truth. They're in the business of a few facts, with a watchdog mentality.

McManus: I have competitors who are serious journalists trying to cover this field, and they are published in dozens and dozens of newspapers. That's evidence that it's possible to penetrate the secular press with a perspective that is different. What we ought to be discussing here is a strategy for a more balanced treatment. That strategy is not going to be one based on belly-aching, which is what I see this study primarily doing.

An awful lot of people grew up hearing, "Don't talk

about religion and politics, it's too controversial." But that's what makes it interesting. Religion and politics are interesting because they're controversial, and yet the controversies are relegated to a fairly minor part of the press, whether television or print.

Robinson: I disagree. I think they cover the controversies in the Church. Now, if you 're telling me that there are only 50 reporters covering religion, I will say I find that shocking and sad. I will also say that in a country that regards itself not so much as committed to spiritualism as to belief in God — and there's a difference — but does see itself committed to the values of the Enlightenment, in which science takes a pre-eminent role, we have no science reporters, and *The Washington Post* only publishes science on Monday in three eight-paragraph pieces with maybe a graph.

My big thing about the press is that it was given a role in fact to be at worst a gadfly, at best a complainant and watchdog. It does that. Is that going to upset traditionalists? Yes. Is it going to upset institutional leaders? Yes. Is it going to upset a lot of people? No question about it.

Does the Church in this country generally do the job it's supposed to do? I think yes. Does the Congress do the job it's supposed to do? I think yes. Does the media do the job I think it's supposed to do? I think they do.

S. Robert Lichter: I want to thank Michael Robinson for providing me with some criticism to respond to. I'm used to getting up to gatherings after having Ben Bradlee describe my work as "asinine," or Carl Bernstein describe it as "ludicrous," or Michael Kinsley describe it as "pseudo-scientific drivel" — these are all direct quotes. So when I hear all this praise, at a certain point I think maybe you're all trying to say nice things about me in the hopes that I'll finally go away without your having to listen to me.

But luckily Michael filled the breach, as I hoped he would, by arguing that there are some problems with this research. Basically, that the glass is really half full rather than half empty, that the coverage isn't all that negative. Secondly, that even if the coverage *is* negative, so what? It's overwhelmed in a tide of popular entertainment that is much more positive. And finally, it doesn't matter because the public image of Catholicism and the Catholic Church is so strongly favorable anyway that you shouldn't worry about any of this.

And it is indeed a half-full, half-empty situation. Coverage is more negative than positive, but it is not overwhelmingly negative. But I must quibble with Michael. In saying "half-empty or half-full," Michael picked the glasses that were the fullest. In saying, let's say, only about one out of 20 CBS stories contained wording describing the Church as oppressive — well, that's true, but one out of six stories in *Time* magazine had that kind of wording. Michael picked the outlet that was least likely to produce that kind of wording.

Similarly, he notes that in fact the coverage was mixed about 45 percent positive to 55 percent negative on opinions about issues of sexual morality. But if you look at issues of authority and dissent in the Church, it was two-to-one negative.

So what Michael says is true, but it's not the whole story. There are emptier glasses in there. And I think the overall conclusion of the study is that on several dimensions of the opinion debate and of the use of language, the Church consistently comes out on the losing or negative side. It's not any *one* thing: we're looking at a pattern of coverage, which is predominantly negative. It's not as negative as George Bush gets, true. It's not as negative as the CIA. It is not as negative as the nuclear power industry or the chemical industry.

But there's a question at a certain point: Is this "as compared to" what — or is it a matter of what should be, regardless of comparisons? If journalism in general has become negativistic and adversarial, does that justify or legitimize negative coverage of a religious institution? I think you have to make a decision about what appropriate coverage is which transcends the scientific: that is, a value judgment about where the line of appropriate coverage lies.

Michael mentions that probably a lot more people will watch Father Dowling on television than read *The New York Times* or even than who watch CBS news in the evening. This is true. However, Father Dowling is the exception that proves the rule. It's a classic case of a religious figure who is brought in to be a detective, who really doesn't do anything to fulfill his religious role, unlike another detective, Father Brown, who actually brought up religious themes. About the only time we see him interacting with religious figures is when his superiors are saying something to the effect, "Shouldn't you be doing something more like a normal priest? Why are you off doing all these strange detective cases?"

I just finished a book on television entertainment. We have done a content analysis — God save us! — of 30 years of television entertainment, and found that in general there are almost no portrayals of religious figures on television. There used to be more. You can go back twenty-five years to "The Flying Nun." You can go back thirty years to "Crossroads," which was an anthology series about priests and ministers ministering to their flocks. Television has become less interested in religious issues over the years.

When you do find religious figures, you get two kinds. Either there are the secularized religious figures, like Father Dowling, or you get religious figures who are fighting against the authority of the Church or against social authority. There were a lot of very positive religious figures during the late 1960s and early 1970s on television. So you did get those kinds of shows. But you don't get that very often on episodic television because you will get protests, and because people like to watch positive characters on television over a period of time.

Even the character of Father Mulcahy in "M.A.S.H." became somewhat more positive as time went on. He was certainly well-meaning if somewhat dithering, and more positive than he was in the original movie, in which he represented one of those awful traditional institutions, like the Army, that we were supposed to shake our fists at.

But you're not going to find on television or in the news media the kind of smoking gun that Brent Bozell waved before us of the actress who exults in her role of getting to spit on a crucifix because it lets her express her deep atheistic principles. What's much more common is a kind of benign neglect — religion is something that *The New York Times* reporters don't talk about much at parties, because they don't run into people who have been to church the weekend before. And particularly they don't run into observant, churchgoing Catholics or into fundamentalist Christians, because those aren't the circles that they run in. They run in cosmopolitan, secular, progressive circles.

Richard Harwood made this point, and I don't think there's any reason for me to belabor it. It's a matter of journalism reflecting to some degree the concerns and understanding and intellectual baggage of the people who are putting together the news product. And obviously, also, reflecting the events that are out there —the reality. But it's also an interaction of the external reality with the internal realities that guide journalists to make something, to give an interpretation to the meaning of these events out there.

Finally, since we have these high favorability ratings, does this matter? Well, once again I wonder if Michael hasn't given us some figures that are almost a little too good to be true. Certainly the Pope is a very popular figure. No one would doubt that, and in fact our study never found anything to suggest consistent negative portrayals of the papacy or of any particular Pope.

As to capturing the entire public image of the Catholic Church by asking about how favorably you regard the Pope, and how favorably you regard "the church" — I did a totally unsystematic, non-scientific survey around my office of the various students and of non-Catholics. Nobody, when asked "What does this mean?" referred to "the church" as "Oh, the Catholic Church." Typically, people would say, "It must be my church," or, "The church of your choice." I think that's very ambiguous question-phrasing. A Catholic would respond "the Catholic Church," but I have it on the words of a Methodist, a Presbyterian and a lapsed Baptist that it is not clear that this is the Catholic Church.

This is a multi-dimensional issue. What I'd like to see are questions that address the kinds of issues we came up with. "Do you regard the Catholic Church as relevant to modern life or out of touch?" "Do you regard the Catholic Church as an institution that is liberating or oppressive?" "How do you feel about the Catholic Church's position on birth control, homosexuality, abortion, the role of Catholic politicians in secular society, etc.?" This issue has many dimensions, and I don't think you can capture them in a single polling question.

Beyond that, of course, to really address what impact the media are having, you need to do the sort of study Michael Robinson has done in the past. You need to do something like a quasi-experimental study, where you actually show people news stories and see if they change their opinions. Or perhaps, if that seems too artificial, do a panel study, where you survey people over time and analyze the content of the news that they're getting, and see if people who get different kinds of news about the Church come out with different attitudes.

In other words, there are various studies aimed at specifically getting at the effects of the news media. If we have those studies, I haven't heard anybody mention them. I'd love to have them. This study, this content analysis, was never intended to do that. It was simply intended to take a look at the Church's media coverage and see what we came up with, and then have the sort of debate we're having now.

But I would like to close with my own feeling about this whole issue, which was expressed pretty well by Richard Harwood. At one point he said "We, the media, reflect and are part of the popular culture, which in the past forty years has exalted to an unprecedented degree individuality, personal freedom, unlimited choices, situational ethics, and anti-establishmentarianism." Now note, he doesn't say, "We in the media are reflecting the views of society, we're a perfect mirror of the society." He's saying, "We're a part of the popular culture." And I believe one of the major cleavages in American life is between a popular culture of news media, television, movies, and idea-disseminators in general who are more cosmopolitan, secular, liberal, than the American public as a whole and are to some degree in conflict with elites from more traditional institutions such as business, military, and traditional religious elites. I think the media are disseminating trends in the larger society and accelerating change in a certain direction which might take place more slowly, or might die aborning, if the media covered these topics in different ways.

Michael Robinson: I am interested in the idea that we have now come to a point in American society where the notion of "the church" doesn't have any meaning to Protestants. Remember, I said that if we come to a situation in which "the church" doesn't mean to Protestants the Catholic Church, it's again an indication that relationships between Catholics and Protestants have become far less conflictual than they used to be. My guess is that in the nineteenth century "the church" would have produced among your students a very direct reaction: "I know what you mean by 'the church' — Romanism."

While I agree with you that we have military elites and business elites and traditional elites different from the Hollywood elites and the Washington press corps, again we come down to the question of effect. At present the only person in America with a higher rating than the Pope is Norman Schwarzkopf, who is strikingly reflective of traditional notions of discipline, patriotism, duty, and that sort of thing. Why? Because he won a war, and he won it on television.

There are now fifty-nine million Catholics in America. They are more numerous than they've ever been, and they're participating in activities in church as well as outside of church. There seems to be a movement away from the more secular churches to the more traditionally-minded churches. There seems to be a movement in the country away from more secular politics to more traditional kinds of political values. I think George Bush was right when he said Republicans are closer to Americans on values than Democrats.

If one sits down with American television, one is going to find a lot of Candice Bergen. Last night I watched her on television, and she was quite modern. She's decided to have a baby out of wedlock, at 42, and she was looking for somebody to support her choice, and actually found no one but the painter. And no one suggested that this was immoral; they just suggested — catch this — "This will cut down on your free time and your time to work around the office." If anything was ever secular, that would be it: "Don't have this baby, Candice Bergen, because then you won't be able to drink with us at the bar after work."

That's on television, but I'm not sure that's the way the country is going. While still committed to the notion of a woman having the right to choose a career, as opposed to just going into the family — my students over the past twenty years have come back to the notion that property matters, that family matters, that the kinds of things that George Bush talks about and Ronald Reagan talked about really matter. . . .

Brian Healy: I will accept the premise that most journalists are today's repository of the Enlightenment attitude that man, through the exercise of reason and effort and good will, can solve all of his problems, rather than the more religious principle that faith and belief can solve your problems. And because of that I think Harwood is correct, in that they bring their own personal consciences — their own personal identification of who they are — to their stories, although most, I believe, will deny that. So I think what happens on positive and negative coverage tends to depend upon the subject, and the reaction of the individual journalist.

I am a practicing Catholic, by the way. I'm also the proud teacher of the fifth-grade class at Sunday school at the Church of Holy Redeemer in Kensington, Maryland. So you should know where I'm coming from. And I am the Senior Producer of the CBS Evening News, and have won Emmy awards, and I was one of the senior producers in charge of our Watergate coverage. Figure that one out.

Let's take a look at the coverage that the press gave the bishops a few years ago when they released their report saying that one had to question the free use of nuclear weapons, that in fact the use of nuclear weapons was probably immoral on most grounds. I would say that on any standard, the Church got a good press. And during the Reagan years, when the bishops issued a report saying the pursuit of wealth at any cost was probably immoral, I think the press received by the bishops was a very positive one. When Pope John Paul II went to Poland for the first time, I was the senior producer of CBS Evening News based in London. They sent me off to Poland, and I would think the Pope received an incredibly good press there. The subject he was talking about was liberalization, in the sense of communism vs. democracy, and about the importance of religious institutions and social institutions.

At the time, the Church in Poland was at an enormously high level of importance to the Polish people. You'll notice that the Church in Poland now is a little less high on the scale of praise, partly because they are getting into the issues that the American Church gets into. When they were defending the rights of freedom, the right to democracy, they were treated differently than when they talk about whether or not you ought to have an abortion, whether you ought to have religious education in all schools, and so on.

Now, appearing on a panel with [Father] Ken Doyle, I said I thought the Church, to many Catholics and many non-Catholics, is defined publicly by the issues on which it has not received such a good press — that is, the reproductive issues. There's no doubt that people know where the Catholic Church stands on the question of abortion. To me, abortion is as divisive in this country as perhaps slavery at one time was. This is an issue everybody has a strong feeling about, and if you're on the other side of the issue — and there's no doubt where most American journalists are — the Church's position, very public and very strong, has earned it a less than positive feeling from many journalists. I think they approach it as a liberalization issue, a freedom issue, an issue of choice. And some journalists approach these issues with fairly strong passions of their own. The press, as a result, does not necessarily give the Church as much due as they should on the roots or the causes for its position on abortion. I think — as a Catholic and not as a journalist, I'm not talking as a CBS official here — that these are defendable.

On the issue of birth control, the Church has had a position which is probably contrary to the personal opinions of most of the journalists I know. On the question of the role of women, many journalists have a view about that. On divorce, a lot of journalists have a strong position on that. So on the gender issues and the reproductive rights issues, the Church will get a different press than it gets on issues that we discussed earlier.

There also is a whole level of issues where the Church gets particularly good coverage without necessarily being seen as "the Church." I mean those individual members of the Church, whether it be nuns or priests, who are doing good works. CBS News has run several stories in the last couple of years on a particular group of nuns who run a homeless shelter in Cincinnati and another in Providence, Rhode Island. You can even talk about the good-natured nun who ended up on CBS Evening News about four weeks ago because she happened to be the national hog-calling champion in America. Here was a person who was open and lovely and caring about the earth and about the life from which she came — small, rural America. That was very positive. But on the sort of hot-button issues we discussed, benign neglect is probably real. That is, the Church isn't perceived by a lot of my colleagues even as a player in a lot of subjects.

For the last six and a half years the executive producer

of CBS Evening News was a graduate of Notre Dame. I was his oldest son's godfather. For the five years before that, it was run by a fellow who also was a practicing Catholic. Don't think we're not there. But just because we *are* there, don't think we consider ourselves Catholic journalists. We consider ourselves journalists who are Catholics. That's why I have a little hesitancy being up here talking about this stuff. Is that fair?

Thomas Troy: Some years ago, out in Kensington, Maryland, I was one of a large number who were greatly troubled by what we considered the bigotry of a particular journalist. The individual was invited out to the Academy of the Holy Cross, to sit on a panel on the subject. What angered all of us, and humiliated all of us, was the journalist's success in putting us on the defensive by accusing us of doing nothing to remedy the defacement of a Jewish synagogue, which had occurred a few weeks earlier, and which literally had no connection with the meeting at hand. We were left on the defensive, and we walked out of the hall — I would say roughly 350 to 400 people — thoroughly annoyed at ourselves.

Now, X number of years later, Michael Robinson comes here with his own message. He tells us that we're not subject to prejudice in the media, that we're doing well, we've got nothing to complain about. And I suddenly find, in large measure, that we are on the defensive. We never had it so good: the most popular Pope in history, the most popular church in history. What on earth are we complaining about?

There's an old philosophical maxim. In the Latin: *Argumentum contra factum non valet.* An argument against the fact is not valid. The fact of the matter is that any practicing, educated, informed Catholic, who belongs to the Knights of Columbus, to the Catholic League, or to any

Catholic organization of any consequence, knows — *knows* in his mind and in his heart that his God, his Christ, his Church, his sacraments, his hierarchy, his priests, his schools, and all his institutions are subject constantly to ridicule and demeaning, not only in news stories but — and here I suggest the Lichter report missed an important thing — in cartoons and in the columnists. Catholics who know anything feel the pain of prejudice and bias. We don't talk about it as a possibility, as a subject for debate. It's rather a subject for action.

Why, as Catholics, are we in this condition? Frank Shakespeare quoted Duff Cooper as saying that there were two churches: the Catholic, and it's wrong, and the others, and they don't matter. I take that very seriously. I think that is a very factual observation. The Catholic Church is a most remarkable institution — not surprising, in view of its divine establishment. It is an institution of fundamental historical, philosophical, theological, and popular significance. If there is any enemy, as far as the secular world is concerned, it is the Catholic Church.

Now, the Catholic Church gets a wonderful press when there is a coronation, when there is a papal visit. The Church is theatrical, the Church provides wonderful material for television. But when the Church takes issue on any fundamental moral political question, it is not viewed as another party to the debate, it is not viewed as another discussant. It is the enemy. It must be destroyed. That's where Catholics feel the discrimination.

What are we going to do about it? Or rather: What *are* we doing about it? Frankly, I find that the Catholic population — 60 million of us, with X number of Representatives, Y number of Senators — is the carpet of American society. The Catholic population has been drummed into silence — the result of two or three hundred years of Anglophilia, of Anglo-Saxon culture. I will give you but one or two examples.

In the last few days we have witnessed the drumming into silence of a graduate of a Catholic college, a Jesuit college, my alma mater — Clarence Thomas — on the idea of natural law. The concept of the natural moral law is fundamental to Catholic, Christian moral philosophy. And would you believe it? This graduate of a Catholic college had not one word of explanation or defense to say about a fundamental principle.

Years ago, Arthur Krock wrote a column whose title I have always remembered. He referred to the superior articulation of the Left. I suggest that Catholics in this country are guilty of the inferior articulation of the Faith. We have in this city two great Catholic universities, the Catholic University of America and Georgetown, presumably staffed by eminent Catholic historians, philosophers, theologians. They never appear here in public. They never appear on television.

A few days ago in the *Washington Times* there was an article on natural law and natural rights. It was written by a Georgetown professor, not a Catholic but a fine man, an Episcopalian, Walter Berns. But he juxtaposed two concepts of the natural law — the Ciceronian and Thomistic on the one hand, the Lockean on the other — and the former he dismissed as a theory which would call for the state imposition of a divinely ordained moral code. That was a regrettable discussion of the difference between the Thomistic concept of the natural law and the Lockean.

I suggest that we do not have an articulate, educated Catholic citizenry here in this very city. Our only voice at the Georgetown University Law School is Eleanor Holmes Norton, who, as I understand it, is trying to get a bill passed by Congress making Operation Rescue, the mounting of a rescue operation, a felony.

In this city, in these newspapers, on these media, Catholic-educated Catholics, somehow or other, never seem able to speak up with any kind of awareness and ability to communicate the inexhaustible wealth of Catholic history. I don't know what, if anything, the Knights and the League and the rest of us are ever going to be able to do about it, until we wake up and realize that we are being unfaithful to the divine commission that is ours.

If you talk about public opinion and return to traditional values and family and so forth, and if you look at public opinion trends in the last 25 years relevant to sexual morality, these are consistently in a liberalizing direction: on abortion, extramarital sex, premarital sex, gay rights, homosexuality. Even on gay rights, while there was a dip after the AIDS epidemic started in public support for legalizing homosexuality, that now has returned to the pre-AIDS levels.

There is a movement in public opinion on private morality that is certainly in the opposite direction from traditional Catholic teachings. Many of these data were cited quite often by political liberals during the Reagan years to argue that people didn't really support Reagan's beliefs even though they were re-electing him.

So, despite the fact that there are Republican Presidents, there are opinion-shifts that are certainly in the opposite direction from the Catholic Church's teachings, and these are very important today in American life.

Robinson: I would concede, although I don't see the polling data moving quite as rapidly as you suggest, that in the area of private decisions concerning sexual morality the country has moved since the Second World War away from what I would consider to be Catholic teaching on morality. [But on] property, family, to some degree religion, I see, in the polls and to some degree in my own students, a movement back to more traditional values. My students think of me as on the losing side. They think that if I voted for Michael Dukakis, my time is past, and I have to understand that those kinds of values are simply no longer in keeping with where American intellectual college students are going. I'm not sure they're going to go where you want them to go, but they are not going in the direction that your media purveyors of popular culture seem over the last few decades to have wanted to take them — if we assume they wanted to take them anywhere.

I also want to say that while I disagree with virtually everything you said, [I do not accept] the idea that there is no articulate spokesperson in America for conservative Catholic history, values, and philosophy — I've heard a couple of very, very articulate people speak today on exactly those issues. I hear a lot of very intelligent conversation from people such as yourself today about where you think the country ought to go.

Patrick Riley: You're addressing Mr. Troy, is that correct?

Robinson: Yes. In fact you were not inarticulate, you were very logical, you were very informed, and you were quite persuasive.

Riley: How much coverage is he going to get in the media?

Robinson: He is not going to get much coverage in the media. He represents an extremist position on the role that the Catholic Church and Catholic people in America should take, given centrist opinion in America. But if he does something truly untoward, if he shoots somebody or throws an egg at somebody, we'll hear something about his philosophy as they try to explain this radical position as part of radical behavior.

But the idea that the Left has a great power of articulation in this country? Who in the American media today speaks for the Left articulately and persuasively? I just don't see that.

Riley: They've all become moderates. Nobody on the Left is left.

Robinson: There is a tendency in our politics for even the Clarence Thomases to become very moderate when push comes to shove on whether or not a confirmation will be voted, or what will result from an election to the presidency or the Senate or House.

The Left doesn't even get listened to in America. It is far more ridiculed than the Right. The system wasn't set up to make sure that Catholic conservatism would prevail in America. But it has a voice, and you certainly have done a better job of giving it voice today than I've heard from secular liberals over the last six months.

III. Historical Background ❦

The Catholic League in Action

Virgil C. Blum, S.J.

THE REVEREND VIRGIL C. BLUM founded the Catholic League for Religious and Civil Rights in 1973 and served as its president until his death in 1990. As a professor of political science, he taught for more than a quarter century, first at Creighton University and then at Marquette University. He authored six books, published more than 200 articles in scholarly journals, popular magazines, and newspapers, and lectured audiences in virtually every major American city. In the following article, he gives reasons why he felt compelled to found the Catholic League, and some examples of its work.

A HIGH SCHOOL student brings home a required social studies booklet, dealing with population control. In a chapter entitled "The Pope's Views on Birth Control," the text concludes that "The world must quickly come to realize that Pope Paul VI has sanctioned the deaths of countless numbers of human beings with his misguided and immoral Encyclical (on artificial birth control)." Discussion questions following the chapter encourage students to consider the possibility of bringing "the Church before a world court or another international tribunal to be tried for crimes against humanity." A college newspaper in your community carries an article satirizing the canonization of Mother Elizabeth Seton. It is entitled "Recently Carnalized Mother Elizabeth Semen: First American Saint." Another college paper carries a cartoon depicting a nun masturbating with a crucifix.

A new community being built is attractive to your family — until you find out a local ordinance will prohibit the construction of church-related schools. You are committed to the value of Catholic education for your children.

All of the above are real incidents. A number of prominent historians agree that anti-Catholicism is a strong factor in American society. Harvard Professor Arthur Schlesinger, Sr., says, "I regard prejudice against [the Catholic] Church as the deepest bias in the history of the American people." According to Johns Hopkins Professor John Higham, "The most luxuriant, tenacious tradition of paranoia agitation in American history has been anti-Catholicism."

To combat anti-Catholicism, the Catholic League was formed. The League, founded in May 1973, can be described as a Catholic counterpart of the Jewish anti-defamation League and the American Civil Liberties Union. It aims to protect Catholic customs, practices, and religious and moral values against defamation by cartoonists, writers, and broadcasters. It aims to defend the religious freedom rights and civil rights of all people. It challenges professions, businesses, and government agencies which engage in discriminatory practices, particularly as they affect religious and ethnic groups.

The League, with a nationwide membership of 18,000, is controlled by a Board of Directors which include constitutional experts, educators, doctors, lawyers, and religious, community, and business leaders. The League is currently involved in cases dealing with civil rights, employment rights, parental rights, and defense against anti-Catholic propaganda. The League's action may be in the form of legal involvement, public protest, financial support or distribution of information.

Defender of Civil Rights

The first legal case in which the League became involved concerned the First Amendment freedom-of-speech rights of Dr. Frank Bolles, a Protestant physician in Boulder, Colorado. As president of a local right-to-life organization, Dr. Bolles sent anti-abortion literature through the mails. For this, the district attorney charged Dr. Bolles with violating a state law which prohibits communications that are "likely to harass or cause alarm."

The Catholic League for Religious and Civil Rights provided legal research and financial assistance for Dr. Bolles' defense.

The trial court ruled in Dr. Bolles' favor, but the appeals court reversed that decision. However, the Colorado Supreme Court said the prosecution of Dr. Bolles violated his right of free speech and unlawfully restricted his full rights of citizenship. In acknowledging the League's support, Dr. Bolles wrote, "I hope that the recent decision regarding our case will give others boldness to speak out in a responsible and appropriate manner, willing to submit our activities to the guidelines of the government by which we live, but not to the point of fearing man and pleasing him rather than God."

In 1974, Kentucky passed a law regulating abortion procedures in that state. The American Civil Liberties Union attacked the constitutionality of the law, and a federal district court ruled all provisions of the statute unconstitutional.

One portion of the Kentucky law stated that "no physician, nurse, staff member or employee of a hospital or other health care facility, who shall state in writing to such hospital or health care facility his objection to performing, participating in, or cooperating in, abortion on moral, religious or professional grounds, be required to, or held liable for refusal to, perform, participate in, or cooperate in such abortion." To protect their rights of conscience as guaranteed in the original law, seven doctors and 21 nurses sought help from the Catholic League.

The League argued that doctors and nurses have the religious and moral right under the First Amendment to refuse to perform or assist in abortions and that the ruling of the district court was in violation of this constitutional right. The court of appeals reversed the district court, upholding the rights of the doctors and nurses.

In another case involving the civil rights of Catholics, the Catholic League had taken initial steps to defend the Sisters of St. Dominic when the State of Washington dropped its case against the motherhouse.

The state had ordered the sisters to bring their motherhouse into code compliance for nursing homes or stop "rendering nursing care" and evict eight elderly sisters. The state contended that the religious women were not members of a family, that they were not "sisters" to each other and therefore not entitled to the rights guaranteed to persons involved in communes, common-law marriages, or other "family" living arrangements.

Sharp public criticism caused the state to drop its case before it reached the courts.

Guardian of Employment Rights

In 1975 a supplement to the Catholic League for Religious and Civil Rights *Newsletter* contained an article by Eugene F. Diamond, M.D., summarizing medical school discrimination against applicants opposed to abortion. The article indicated 21 of 60 schools surveyed questioned prospective students about abortion; another 18 left such questions to the prerogative of interviewers. Two schools admitted that applicants who stated they would refuse to participate in an abortion would be rejected; another 13 schools said such statements would cause "administrative problems" in the application process.

As a result of the article, Sen. Richard S. Schweiker (R.-Pa.) in 1977 introduced a bill to prevent medical schools from discriminating against applicants opposed to abortion. "It is the law of the land that no federal money can go to any school which discriminates on the basis of race or religion," Schweiker said. "It is deeply disturbing that some medical schools are discriminating on the basis of an opinion founded on religious or moral grounds."

Protector of Parents' Rights

On behalf of concerned parents in Lansing, Michigan, the Catholic League for Religious and Civil Rights began a lawsuit challenging the right of a state agency to give young teenagers birth control instruction and contraceptive devices without parental knowledge or consultation.

A federal court ruled against the practice. The judge based his decision on the role of the family as "the primary and essential cell of our society." He said "deception of parents" would increase the tension and intensify the normal strain on family ties generally associated with adolescence. Under the ruling, minors whose parents refuse to let them have contraceptives may appeal their parents' decision to the juvenile court.

In another case involving parental rights, plans for Pontchartrain-New Town, Louisiana, a federally financed community for 90,000 people, prohibited the building of church-related schools.

The Catholic League confronted James Lynn, then Secretary of the Department of Housing and Urban Development. The League demanded that the rights of parents to choose the education their children would receive be respected and guaranteed in New Town or the League would begin legal action to insure the protection of these rights.

When the story of the Catholic League-HUD confrontation hit the press, Lynn immediately said he would not approve a New Town proposal that violated the constitutional rights of parents.

The League also retained a lawyer to defend the rights of Episcopalian parents in Washington, D.C., to build an Episcopal school. When the parents sought a building permit for the school, opponents of church-related education argued before the local zoning commission that it could not grant a permit without the approval of local public school officials and an assessment of the impact of the Episcopal school on nearby public schools.

The League's lawyer argued that such a requirement would violate the First Amendment rights of parents in the education of their children, and the zoning commission agreed.

Watchdog of Anti-Catholic Propaganda

The League's activities are not limited to legal issues. It takes swift and widespread action in defending the image of the Catholic Church and its members.

The *National Lampoon* devoted practically its entire December 1974 issue to the most crude and vicious sort of mockery of religious beliefs and persons. The Catholic, Protestant, and Jewish faiths were all subjected to blasphemy and ridicule in cartoons and text.

In January 1976 *Penthouse* magazine printed a crude caricature of Terence Cardinal Cooke. An accompanying joke expressed concern for the cardinal's emotional health, supposedly caused by his reaction to reports of President John F. Kennedy's alleged affair with Judith Exner. A fictitious aide to Cooke pointed out, "It's not the affair that's bothering him, it's Mrs. Exner's revelation that — instead of using the church-approved method of birth control — the president employed artificial means of contraception."

In both incidents, the League's response was the same — to write major advertisers questioning their support of such publications. As a result, six national advertisers canceled their advertising campaigns in the *National Lampoon*. The reaction of *Penthouse* advertisers was less cooperative, although several registered the League's complaint with the magazine.

Protests by the Catholic League for cartoons and articles contained in college publications have resulted in greater concern over student journalism practices. The student newspaper of Harrisburg (Pa.) Community College printed an article satirizing the canonization of Mother Elizabeth Seton. After the League protested, the acting president of the college issued an apology and noted "We have taken steps to assure that such articles do not appear again . . . we have instituted a new credit course on campus which will emphasize journalistic ethics."

A student newspaper at City College of New York carried a cartoon depicting a nun masturbating with a crucifix. Although complaints from the League to the district attorney resulted only in a comment that "the whole paper had to be analyzed," the president of the college agreed to "prevent the repetition of such offensive, insensitive, and degrading material." Appropriate standards for student journalism was placed on the agenda of the college's policy advisory committee.

In another case, a cartoon depicting a peasant woman kneeling before a statue of the Blessed Mother with the caption, "Little Virgin, you who conceived without sinning, teach me to sin without conceiving," appeared on the front cover of a booklet distributed in Panama by the U.S. Agency for International Development (AID). The Catholic League protested against the use of tax funds for such anti-Christian defamatory material. The result of the complaint and subsequent publicity "raised Cain in the Congressional Record," according to the League's executive director.

In cooperation with other Catholic agencies, the League vigorously protested against rebroadcasts of CBS's "Maude" pro-abortion episodes. The League argued that, since the airwaves belong to the people, the people have a right to know both sides of a controversial issue.

Thirty-nine CBS affiliates refused to re-broadcast the episodes, and only one of the six minutes allotted for advertising was sold by the network.

Where Do We Stand; What Do We Do?

Many Catholics do not want to recognize, particularly in this ecumenical age, that there is anti-Catholicism in America. Anti-Catholic prejudice today is generally much more subtle and more difficult to challenge. No longer are signs posted in shop windows, "Irish need not apply."

That, of course, does not make today's kind of prejudice any less objectionable, or un-Christian, or un-American. Objective analysts of our society note that anti-Catholicism still exists in our society. The Department of Labor stated in the *Federal Register:* "Experience has indicated that . . . Catholics . . . continue to be excluded from executive, middle management, and other job levels because of discrimination based on their religion."

These charges of anti-Catholic prejudice can be supported by massive (but not extensive) collection of factual data. Such data have been collected showing discrimination against Catholics in universities, business, law firms, federal courts, and industry.

While the mass media today aggressively reports discrimination against blacks, women, and Jews, it rarely reports the facts about discrimination against Catholics and particularly against Catholic ethnics.

What can we do? Alone, we can register our lonely protests against anti-Catholic materials, practices, and policies. But one or ten or one hundred persons fighting an establishment brings few results. Power comes with numbers and organization, with knowledge and expertise, with financial and legal resources.

The Catholic League for Religious and Civil Rights offers this type of power to the Catholic community. We believe that Catholics, like other Christians, have the right and duty to bring the message of Christ into the social and political marketplace. In our society, this duty can only be fulfilled by active membership in interest groups that directly concern themselves with religious and moral issues, with the defamation of the customs, practices, and values of the Catholic faith, with the religious and civil rights of Catholics and others, and with the right of the Catholic Church to teach and to minister to the spiritual needs of its people.

Anti-Catholicism and the Knights of Columbus

Christopher J. Kauffman

CHRISTOPHER J. KAUFFMAN is the Catholic Daughters of the Americas Professor of Church History at the Catholic University of America. He is also editor of the U.S. Catholic Historian. Among Dr. Kauffman's publications are <u>Faith and Fraternalism: The History of the Knights of Columbus 1882-1982</u> and the six-volume <u>Makers of the American Catholic Community: Historical Studies of the American People in the United States 1789-1989</u> for which he was general editor.

I.

AN EARLY 1992 cover of *Time* magazine featuring photos of Ronald Reagan and Pope John Paul II and carrying the legend "Holy Alliance. . . ." was not inherently an anti-Catholic portrayal;[1] nor was Carl Bernstein's accompanying article intended to contribute to an historical caricature of corrupt papal *realpolitik*. But, if those responsible for *Time*'s cover had ridden the Washington, D.C., Metro system during the previous two years, they very likely would have noted a paid ad in subway cars almost identical to their cover: photos of the President and the Pope, with the caption "Who Is Running the Country?" The ad's anonymous sponsors, whom I perceive as perpetuating the old myth concerning a papal conspiracy to undermine our republic and its Constitution, must have been delighted to see the cover of *Time* "imitating" their Metro rendering of an unholy conspiracy.

In this overview I shall explore the historical development of this strand of political anti-Catholicism as it was woven into the print media's portrayal of the "Romanist menace." After a brief glance at the various forms of nineteenth-century anti-Catholicism, the focus will be on the period 1910-1917 when the Knights of Columbus established itself as a premier Catholic anti-defamation society.

Anti-Catholicism developed in a dialectical context. The Catholic Church's struggle against the impact of the French Revolution placed it on the side of monarchy's reaction to democracy. Catholic militancy in the United States exacerbated tensions; Catholics could exaggerate their victimization, though their experience was never as violent or as severe as the black experience of racism nor as continuous as the Jewish experience of anti-Semitism.

II.

The animus toward Catholics in the United States has its roots in a blend of historical Protestant-Catholic tensions, to which both denominations contributed, and the Enlightenment's identification of Catholicism with superstition, with the corrupt union of crown and altar and with traditional authoritarianism's strategy to sabotage democratic movements.[2]

The economic component of anti-Catholicism is nativism, that xenophobic reaction to immigration that has manifested itself from the Irish "invasion" during the 1830s and 1840s to the Latino and Asian incursions during the final third of the twentieth century. "No popery" was the cry of the political zealots, while the guardians of the economy decried the proliferation of pauperism (today's welfarism) and the immigrants' tendencies toward violence. In the latter half of the nineteenth century the Molly Maguires in the coal field, the Haymarket rioters in Chicago, and the Knights of Labor throughout the nation were viewed as manifestations of the uncivilized and animalistic behavior associated with European Catholic decadence and class warfare. There is a paradox in the two portrayals of the Catholic laity, at once "priest-ridden" automatons and savage socialists and anarchists.[3]

A cultural anti-Catholicism, frequently laced with political and economic hostility, was vented by the bogus escaped nuns, such as Maria Monk, ostensibly the author of *The Awful Disclosures by Maria Monk of the Hotel Dieu Nunnery of Montreal*, or the ex-priest, such as Ricardo, the major character in a recently published picture story (comic book) by a putatively "Christian" publishing house. In such popular media (Maria Monk's "exposé," considered the *Uncle Tom's Cabin* of Know-Nothingism, sold 300,000 copies by 1861), convents and seminaries are portrayed as prisons of perversion. With various forms of the media depicting the pope as an anti-Christ, immigrant laity as a blend of docility, shiftlessness, and violence, and priests and nuns as depraved and tyrannical, the Know Nothings of the 1850s had all the "evidence" necessary to attempt to deprive Catholics of political rights and equal opportunity.[4]

The American Protective Association's reaction of the 1880s and 1890s to the political ascendancy of the immigrants, symbolized by the election of Catholic mayors in three New England towns in the 1880s, resuscitated the

Know-Nothing creed, code, and cult. The APA also launched a severe attack upon Catholic education. The parochial school was viewed as elitist, separatist, and papist, that is, inherently anti-American. Newspapers dominated by the APA invoked the mythical little red schoolhouse as a symbol of the only rite of passage to American citizenship. In this sense, Catholic citizenship was an oxymoron.[5]

(Since this overview suffers from its general character, it is important to point out that, of course, there were many people of good will who refused to identify with the anti-Catholic animus.)

III.

A unique blend of faith and fraternalism, the Knights of Columbus is the largest organization of Catholic laity in the world. Since its founding in 1882, it has responded to the myriad needs of the local churches in the United States, Canada, Mexico, Puerto Rico, and the Philippines. Michael J. McGivney, the New Haven, Connecticut, priest who established the Knights of Columbus, implicitly fostered an American Catholic apologetic, one which extolled the harmony between religious liberty and Catholicism. Father McGivney's gifts were many and various. He was an unassuming, pious priest who easily elicited the trust of the laity. Concerned with the strong appeal of the prohibited secret societies among Catholic youth and with the plight of the widows and children who had suffered the loss of the breadwinner, he was eager to form a fraternal insurance society imbued with deep loyalties to Catholicism and to the American experience.[6]

After many meetings, McGivney and a small group of laymen decided to establish an independent society rather than become a branch of one or two existing Catholic benefit societies. In early February 1882, they placed their fledgling fraternal order under the patronage of Christopher Columbus. According to the few surviving documents, the Columbian motif represented several facets of the group's Catholic consciousness. Columbus was the symbol *par excellence* of the Catholic contribution to American culture. By portraying the navigator's landing at San Salvador as the Catholic baptism of the nation, the Knights were asserting religious legitimacy. Just as the heirs of the Pilgrims invoked the Mayflower as the Protestant symbol of their identity as early Americans, so the Knights invoked the *Santa Maria* as the symbol of their self-understanding as Catholic citizens.

One of the charter members of the Order referred to the cause of Catholic civil liberty when he asserted that the Order's patron signified that, as Catholic descendants of Columbus, "[We] were entitled to all rights and privileges due to such a discovery by one of our faith."[7] In short, the founders perceived Columbus as a cultural symbol that instilled a sense of Catholic pride. The term Knight conveyed a commitment to struggle against nativism and anti-Catholicism as "Catholic gentlemen," a descriptive term frequently used by the Knights which reveals a portion of their social identity. Because the Irish immigrants had been caricatured as rowdy drunks, the Irish-American drive for respectability was manifested in this term, Catholic gentlemen. Ever conscious of nativist and anti-Catholic biases, the Knights proudly displayed their worthiness as citizens and zealously defended the loyalty of their Church.

Columbianism was expressed in persistently optimistic and idealistic terms; but, given the K. of C. consciousness of the ever-present threat from the forces of anti-Catholicism, Columbianism was also, of necessity, a rallying ground for the defense of the faith. The optimism of the progressive era was countered by those groups which feared the increased immigration from southern and eastern Europe (which totaled nearly seven million between 1897 and 1914) would ultimately result in the breakdown of "American" folkways. Anglo-Saxon nativism included anti-Semitism, widespread antagonism to Italian and Slavic peoples, a resurgence of racism in the South and North, and the growth of anti-Oriental sentiment in the West and Northwest, symbolized by the canard of the "Yellow Peril." This type of nativism was in the ascendant by 1910, when the new immigration reached its peak, and was expressed in secular, even scientific, terms. Primarily aimed at immigrant restriction, it was popular among urban middle and upper classes. It did not spill out as overt anti-Catholicism, because by this time these classes had developed a secular perspective through which to filter their anti-foreigner animus.[8]

The anti-Catholicism which emerged around 1910 was centered in small rural towns where traditional Protestant prejudices lingered. While the American Protective Association had feared Catholicism as a menace to both liberty and capitalism (Catholic immigrants were equated with anarchists), the new religious xenophobia was popularized by those who felt Progressive reforms had failed because of a grand papal conspiracy. The historian John Higham suspects that the new anti-Catholic sentiment "came from a displacement or distortion or antimonopolistic sentiment. . . . It is hard to explain the rebirth of anti-Catholic ferment except as an outlet for expectations which Progressivism raised and then failed to fulfill."[9]

One such frustrated progressive, Wilbur Franklin Phelps, became an impassioned spokesman of the new anti-Catholicism, which he vented in his weekly newspaper, *The Menace*. Founded in the Ozark town of Aurora, Missouri, in 1911, *The Menace* waged incessant war on Catholicism. Because the Knights of Columbus had become such a strongly visible Catholic organization, the Order became a symbol of Rome's alleged menace to American political liberty and social reform. Thomas Watson, also a frustrated reformer, became, by 1910, a major figure in the new anti-Catholic campaign through the medium of *Watson's Magazine*. He, too, viewed the Knights of Columbus as a sort of fifth column in the papal conspiracy to persecute heretics — that is, all Protestants — and to abolish American liberty.[10] (Watson's anti-Semitism was even more vehement.)

In his 1913 New Year's greeting to his brother Knights, Supreme Knight James Flaherty noted the rise of anti-Catholicism. "Only a few years ago we had reason to resent the unkindness, in some cases cowardly conduct, shown to our Church and its children. In the future we will have to fight the enemies of our Church in connection with great questions touching taxation, education, divorce, and socialism. We will be fair, always fair and our enemies will find us in the open . . . the future is to be ours but, as counsellor, I can give no better advice, to every council in our Order, than is conveyed by the word 'Prepare.' "[11]

Though Flaherty did not elaborate on the anti-Catholic aspect of socialism, the editor of the *Columbiad*, D. P. Toomey, lashed out at the "foul socialist publication, *The Menace*," in the same issue in which Flaherty's article appeared.[12] The *Catholic Columbian*, a K. of C. publication of Columbus, Ohio, also linked *The Menace* to socialism: "Seeing that the Catholic Church is the greatest obstacle to the success of materialistic and anti-Christian socialism, socialists have started *The Menace* to destroy the Catholic

Church. *The Menace* is simply the tool of socialism."[13]

The Knights' struggle against *The Menace* and *Watson's Magazine* engendered the creation of the bogus Fourth Degree oath that entered the election of 1912. Besides the political invective against papal aggression — the Knights were "in the militia of the Pope" — this oath includes a passage whereby the Knights swore by "the blessed Sacrament" to "wage relentless war, secretly and openly, against all heretics, Protestants, and Masons [and] . . . extirpate them from the face of the earth" by such vile means as to "hang, burn, waste, flog, boil, strangle and bury alive these infamous heretics."[14] Despite its absurdity, the oath was circulated by *The Menace* and quoted in the media from Newfoundland to California, and even surfaced during the presidential campaign of John F. Kennedy, a Fourth Degree Knight.[15] The Order's immediate response was to prosecute on charges of criminal libel all those who distributed the oath. Though such cases entailed enormous time and energy, this proved to be a moderately effective deterrent.[16]

Another manifestation of the Order's anti-defamation character was the 1914 establishment of the Knights of Columbus Commission on Religious Prejudices. Under the chairmanship of Patrick Henry Callahan, then K. of C. state deputy of Kentucky and a wealthy industrialist well known for his capital-labor profit-sharing plan, the commission followed its mandate to the letter. It was charged "to study the causes, investigate conditions and to suggest remedies for the religious prejudice that has been manifest through press and rostrum in a malicious and scurrilous campaign that is hostile to the spirit of American freedom and liberty and contrary to God's law of 'Love thy neighbor as thyself.' "[17]

The commission sponsored an education campaign by

"informing and correcting editors and journalists who allowed religious prejudices to surface in their newspapers" and supporting the Department of Justice in its criminal libel prosecutions against "bigoted publications."[18]

Callahan also pursued people of goodwill to associate with the commission's goals. He successfully recruited several Protestant clergymen, including the father of the Social Gospel, Washington Gladden. A Congregationalist minister, Gladden had composed an article published in *Harpers* entitled "Anti-Papal Panic" in which he severely criticized the APA and lashed out at the revival of anti-Catholicism.[19]

The commission's investigation of the causes of religious prejudices was further refined during its second year. "Religious prejudices have come down to us through many generations, from centuries of enmity and strife when Catholics and Protestants took turns persecuting one another and together persecuted the Jews."[20] The commission distinguished between individual bias, considered endemic to human nature, and social prejudice, the product of "conditions and circumstances in our country, whose democratic form of government has given rise to any number of popular movements."[21]

Callahan broadened the scope of the commission during its third year by establishing a clearinghouse for "the exchange and dissemination" of projects, programs, and publications related to the promotion of the commission's opposition to religious prejudice. However, when the United States entered World War I in April 1917, the commission decided to terminate its work at the close of the fraternal year on June 30. In his introduction to the commission's final report, Callahan summarized its purpose, its strategies, and the character and tone of its operations. After noting again the distinction between individual and social prejudice, he confidently stated that the commission had contributed to the demise of the latest anti-Catholic movement. "For the first time in the history of anti-Catholic campaigns one of them has been peacefully broken at high tide."[22]

The commission had persistently viewed the "professional propagandists" as the central force of the campaign. To show how this force had lost its momentum, Callahan pointed out that between August 1914, when the Commission on Religious Prejudices was established, and January 1917, the number of anti-Catholic publications dropped from 60 to two or three. He pointed to the absence of bigotry in the national elections of 1916 and to the fact that few anti-Catholic bills were introduced in state legislatures in 1916 as further illustrations of the weakness of the movement. He credited the commission's success to the dignified way in which it had comported itself, elevating the discussion of religious prejudices from the heated arena of passion and bitter invective to the dignified realm of "sane, calm, composed discussion," and recommended that "the commission ought to be discontinued because its work is done, and, we venture to think, not altogether badly done. Not that bigotry is dead, not by any means, that will never be. But the wave of bigotry that a little while ago was spreading over the country has subsided and its bitter waters lie stagnant."[23]

For three years the Commission on Religious Prejudices had waged a national campaign against anti-Catholicism with studious respectability and candor. It rationalized its efforts not along the lines of a defense of the Church, which it explicitly stated needed no *apologia*, but rather on the basis of the constitutional guarantees of freedom of religion. Callahan's wealth allowed him the time to respond vigorously to every manifestation of religious prejudice. His boundless energy was expressed in a variety of causes, but none took precedence over his commitment to enlighten those who were subject to the cant of the professional anti-Catholic propagandists. As a Catholic social reformer who implemented his own profit-sharing scheme, Callahan seems to have been very confident of the role of personal initiative in the solution of social problems.

The Commission on Religious Prejudices was the order's first institutional manifestation of its traditional characteristic as a Catholic anti-defamation society. Though both the B'nai B'rith's Anti-Defamation League and the Knights of Columbus Commission on Religious Prejudices aimed to enlighten the public on the un-American character of religious discrimination, the commission dissolved because it had concluded that the anti-Catholic movement had reached its nadir as a force in society, while the Anti-Defamation League has continued to struggle against anti-Semitism, which has been firmly embedded in American social attitudes. However, in the 1920s the Knights once again found themselves confronting a revival of anti-Catholicism, and though the Order did not re-establish the commission, its anti-defamation character was strongly expressed in a massive struggle against the most virulent anti-Catholic organization, the Ku Klux Klan.

IV.

In his classic work *Strangers in the Land*, John Higham entitles his treatment of the conflicts during the postwar period "The Tribal Twenties."[24] The immigrant restriction law of 1924 had closed the gates while the Ku Klux Klan was waging a national campaign that included the revival of the bogus K. of C. oath, attempts to force all children to attend public schools, and a political and economic agenda that harked back to the Know Nothings.[25] The Knights of

Columbus responded by supporting the litigation in the famous Oregon School Case and by establishing its Historical Commission's Racial Contribution Series. Aimed at nativism, the series published books on the contributions of the Jews, the Germans, and African-Americans; this last edition was written by W. E. B. DuBois.[26]

Unlike the pre-war anti-Catholicism that viewed the Church as responsible for the failure of social reform, the animus of the twenties was directed at the urban dominance of the 'hyphenated' Americans, the Catholic foreigners in the cities who were threatening the Protestant way of life. The KKK understood itself as the last line of defense of 100 percent Christian Americanism.

The Knights' anti-defamation projects included a major political effort against religious persecution in Mexico during the 1920s and 1930s and a widespread series of responses to Paul Blanshard's 1940s and 1950s attacks upon the American Catholic hierarchy as foreign agents of the pope. Blanshard characterized the latter as "a world monarch who rules a synthetic moral empire that overlaps and penetrates the sovereignty of all earthly governments."[27]

Certain of the themes in Blanshard's *American Freedom and Catholic Power* have been the principal political pollutants in the mainstream of anti-Catholicism for over 200 years. They were implied in the rhetorical question posed by the subway advertisement which I mentioned at the start of this overview: "Who is running America?" In the 1990s, political, economic, and cultural anti-Catholicism persist; there are even manifestations of anti-Catholic pornography. From the time of Father Michael McGivney to today, the Knights of Columbus have responded to the anti-Catholic animus as Catholic gentlemen committed to the high road of moral leadership and the elevation of discourse to the level of civility.

Endnotes

1. *Time* 138 (February 24, 1992), cover.
2. For this [section] the following works have been consulted: Robert N. Bellah and Frederick E. Greenspahn, *Uncivil Religion: Interreligious Hostility in America* (New York, 1987); Ray Allen Billington, *The Protestant Crusade, 1800-1860: A Story of the American Origins of Nativism* (New York, 1938); Jay P. Dolan, *The American Catholic Experience* (New York, 1987); John Tracy Ellis, *Documents in American Catholic History* (Wilmington, Delaware, 1987) vols. I, II; Paul J. Folk, *Pioneer Catholic Journalism* (reprint, New York, 1969); Andrew Greeley, *An Ugly Little Secret: Anti-Catholicism in North America* (Kansas City, 1977); James Hennesey, S.J., *American Catholics: A History of the Roman Catholic Community in the United States* (New York, 1981); John Higham, *Strangers in the Land: Patterns of American Nativism*, 1860-1920 (New Brunswick, N.J., 1955); John Kane, *Catholic-Protestant Conflicts in America* (Chicago, 1955); Martin E. Marty, ed., *The Religious Press in America* (Westport, Ct., 1963); David O'Brien, *Public Catholicism* (New York, 1989).
3. Donald Kinzer, *An Episode in Anti Catholicism: The American Protective Association* (Seattle, 1964), p. 30. Also see Higham, pp. 32-48.
4. Higham, pp. 102-09.
5. Kinzer, pp. 45-46. As a result of the perception that Grover Cleveland's election depended on the Catholic vote, the Reverend Mr. Burchard coined the 3R's of anti-Catholic animus: "Rum, Romanism and Rebellion."

See Kinzer, p. 19.

6. Christopher J. Kauffman, *Faith and Fraternalism*, New York, 1982), pp. 1-28.
7. M. C. O'Connor's Recollections, manuscript, archives of the Knights of Columbus (hereafter cited AKC).
8. Higham, p. 17.
9. *Ibid.*, p. 179.
10. I*Ibid.*, pp. 179-80. Also see Kauffman, p. 168.
11. James A. Flaherty, "Future of the Knights of Columbus, *Columbiad* XXI (October, 1914), p. 4.
12. Editorial "A Fearless Knight's Triumph" *Columbiad* XX (January, 1913), p. 4.
13. "A Tool of Socialism," a report from the *Catholic Columbian* (Columbus, Ohio), in *Columbiad* XX (April, 1913), p. 10.
14. Reprint of the Bogus Oath, Bogus Oath File, AKC.
15. "Injunction Issued Against Circulation of Bogus Knights of Columbus Oath," *Columbiad* XL (October, 1960), pp. 16, 38.
16. *Criminal Libels Against the Knights of Columbus Exposed* (New Haven, Ind).
17. "Supreme Knight's Report," *Columbiad* XXI (September, 1914), p. 32.
18. *Report of Commission on Religious Prejudices* (New Haven, 1915), p. 4.
19. Washington Gladden, "Anti-Papal Panic" reprint from *Harper's, Columbiad* XXI (August, 1914), pp. 4, 13.
20. *Report of the Commission on Religious Prejudices* (New Haven, 1916), p. 21.
21. I*Ibid.*, p. 22.
22. *Report of Commission on Religious Prejudice* (New Haven, 1917), p. 3.
23. I*Ibid.*, p. 5.
24. Higham, pp. 264-99.

25. On the Ku Klux Klan see David M. Chalmers, *Hooded Americanism, The First Century of the Ku Klux Klan* (New York, 1965) and Kenneth T. Jackson, *The Ku Klux Klan in the City, 1915-1930* (New York, 1967).
26. Kauffman, pp. 269-73.
27. Paul Blanshard, *American Freedom and Catholic Power* (Boston, 1958), p. 48.

IV. Editors ❧

PATRICK RILEY, holder of a doctorate in philosophy from the Pontifical University of St. Thomas Aquinas in Rome, is Director of Governmental Affairs for the Catholic League for Religious and Civil Rights in Washington, D.C. For a dozen years he was roving correspondent, based in Rome, of the Catholic News Service, and his articles have appeared on several continents and in several languages.

RUSSELL SHAW is Director of Public Information and Director of Publications for the Knights of Columbus, Washington, D.C. He has published many articles, columns, and reviews, and is the author or co-author of eleven works of fiction, moral theology, spirituality, and social commentary.